British
Horror Films
That Time Forgot

Thomas Baxter

Contents

AUTHOR'S NOTE

Everyone has watched things like The Wicker Man or Shaun of the Dead or Don't Look Now. Many of us have watched all the Amicus and Hammer films. However, there are many films in the long history of British horror which are either obscure or simply somewhat forgotten. Have you, for example, ever watched Unmasked Part 25? Xtro II? How about Screamtime or Bloodstream? Have you ever sat through The House That Vanished or Persecution? What about Sleepwalker or The Shout? In this book we will shine a light on some of the lesser viewed films in the history of the British horror industry.

I should point out that this book eschews the cavalcade of British horror films which have been inflicted on us in more recent years. There are so many of these VOD and straight to DVD type films it is nearly impossible to keep track and a large number of them are nigh on unwatchable. That would be a book in and of itself. It is not really applicable to call (to pluck something at random) a film like Strippers vs Werewolves a 'forgotten' horror film in the way that you might call Symptoms a forgotten horror film. Films like Strippers vs Werewolves were forgotten the second they were birthed into existence. Old films are often fascinating for the British horror fan to 'discover' - which assuredly can't be said of newer films in the vein of Strippers vs Werewolves. We will though go up to 2011 in this book in order to discuss the doomed Wicker Man sequel.

Some of the films in this book are excellent (Symptoms, Full Circle, Unman, Wittering and Zigo, Paperhouse etc) and some of the films in this book are terrible (I'm looking directly at you Incense for the Damned). Going through them all though, even the bad ones, was a lot of fun. One last thing I should add is that my thoughts on the films which follow are merely of course my own opinion. You may enjoy some of these films more than I did and you may not love all the ones that I loved. It's down down to personal taste.

Vampire motorcycles, devil dolls, killer chimps, escaped lunatics, lighthouse horrors, troglodytes in caves, Satanic sacrifice in an antiques shop, demon babies who don't want to be born, teleportation shenanigans cursed by a fly, frozen Nazis, video nasties, zombies in Cornwall, louche vampire cults, necrophile killers, human/plant hybrid horrors, dream demons, murderous Punch & Judy men, killer garden gnomes, outer space terror, murderous priests, mansion mysteries, woodland secrets, ghosts, Christmas splatter fests, babysitters in peril. All this and much more awaits in the British Horror Films That Time Forgot...

THE APPOINTMENT (1982)

The Appointment was directed Lindsey C. Vickers - who worked on some of the Hammer films and had previously directed a short film called The Lake. The frustrating treatment of The Appointment meant he never directed anything again - which is a shame. The Appointment was financed by the National Coal Board Pension Fund and was proposed as one of a number of television films which would make up a sort of anthology series. The other films did not transpire though and The Appointment did not get a cinema release. It was available on home video for a time but then became a lost film that had been completely forgotten. Thankfully it was recently rediscovered and given a DVD release.

The film takes place in the Home Counties. It begins with a schoolgirl named Sandy (Auriol Goldingham) walking home along a footpath by the woods after school. She's part of the school orchestra and carries a violin case. Voices call out to her from the woods, which make her nervous, and all of a sudden she's violently dragged away by an unseen force. Holy cripes. This scene is terrifying. What an opening! These early scenes have a voiceover of a police officer reading the reports on Sandy's disappearance. They soon drop the voiceover though. You think that the film is going to be about the mystery of what happened to Sandy but it isn't at all. The film then changes into a strange and sometimes unfathomable psychological drama.

The Appointment is always weirdly compelling though and plays a bit like a very bizarre episode of Hammer House of Mystery & Suspense. What is the main plot of The Appointment? Ian (the great Edward Woodward in a very large pair of glasses) lives in a nice house with his wife Dianna (Jane Merrow) and fourteen year-old daughter Joanne (Samantha Weysom). Joanne seems to have a very close bond with her father and is devastated when she learns he can't attend her school music concert (she's a talented violinist) because he has to attend some sort of work related meeting many miles away. Joanne throws a giant strop and although Ian feels guilty to miss the recital he decides he has no choice because the work related meeting is very important.

That night Ian dreams about his car being attacked by Rottweilers. His wife also has strange dreams. On his long drive to his meeting, Ian seems to keep encountering a lorry with Rottweilers on the side. Meanwhile, we see Joanne talking to something unseen by the (now fenced off) area of the woods where Sandy vanished. What can any of this mean?

The Appointment is not one of those films that gives you all the answers so you have to fill in some of the blanks for yourself. It seems pretty obvious though that Joanne has some sort of psychic ability - or dark powers. There is an obvious link between Sandy and Joanne which may (or may not) be significant.

The film also appears to suggest that there might be something unhealthy going on between Ian and his daughter in that she is very possessive of him. Ian goes to enter Joanne's room at night but then decides not to. It seems unlikely that this subtext was unwitting or unintentional. Samantha Weysom (who has no acting credits beyond 1991) gives a rather bizarre performance with an odd (and wooden) line delivery but you know what? It actually works for the character. It makes Joanne seem weird.

It is sometimes said that this film is not horror and has no gore but that's not true. It has a consistently unsettling atmosphere thanks to the sound effects and score and a mechanic meets a very nasty end at one point. The film jumbles up dreams and reality in an effective way so sometimes you aren't quite sure what is real. Much of the film is just Edward Woodward driving in his car and, blimey, what a journey. It seems as if he drives halfway around the world! I bet part of the appeal for Edward Woodwood in taking this film was that he'd get to sit down for most of it! Why not just take the train? He'd surely get to his destination quicker.

The car crash sequence near the end is utterly brilliant. It's sort of ridiculous at first but then becomes terrifying when the car flips up over a precarious drop. The sequence where Ian is all bloodied and dazed and trapped in his car (which is perched in trees!) is both gripping and frightening. There's some nice outdoor location work in the driving scenes. Woodward earns his money with this crash sequence alone. The Appointment is a fascinating thriller/horror that deserved a wider audience. It's a shame really that it didn't get more attention. It would have made a great episode in either of the 1980s Hammer television shows. This film might be a bit slow for some but it is worth sticking with and is one of those films that lingers in the memory for a while after you've seen it.

BLOODBATH AT THE HOUSE OF DEATH (1984)

Bloodbath at the House of Death was directed by Ray Cameron - who wrote the film with Barry Cryer. This was ostensibly a vehicle for the comedian and radio presenter Kenny Everett and made by the creative team from his television show. In the film Kenny is Dr Lukas Manderville, the head of a team of scientists who investigate Headstone Manor, a reputedly haunted residence where dark things once happened. Needless to say there are soon spooky shenanigans aplenty as blood sloshes around and people are bumped off...

I can't say I'm the biggest fan of spoof parody horror films. Naturally, you have your gold standard in Young Frankenstein and Shaun of the Dead and ones that were enjoyable enough (like Carry On Screaming and A House in Nightmare Park) but a great many horror spoofs are absolutely tedious to sit through.

Sadly, Bloodbath at the House of Death falls firmly into the tedious category. This film fails to mimic the atmosphere and style of the films it is attempting to spoof and it also fails to make you laugh. So you have the worst of all worlds. A badly made horror parody with a terrible script. In this desperately unfunny film the jokes land with an audible thud as tumbleweed blows past in the background.

The best part of the film is the massacre at the start because it feels the most like watching a straight horror film from this era. Once that is over with the film falls off a cliff - unless that is you like endless fart jokes and Kenny Everett doing a comedy German accent. Someone will shriek in the film to look out for a bat and then get hit by a cricket bat. These are the sort of jokes you get in Bloodbath at the House of Death. At one point a character investigates the house to the strains of spooky music. When he opens the toilet it turns out Dr Manderville is sitting in there with a cello playing the spooky music. You can see these jokes coming a mile off.

It is probably unfair to be too harsh on the shortcomings of Bloodbath at the House of Death because it was clearly made with little money (and probably quickly too) but this is a curiously flat and tame affair for a horror spoof made in the early 1980s at the height of the video nasty era. You always hope that Bloodbath at the House of Death is going to be more outrageous when it comes to gore and sexploitation but it never really is. You have a few bits of nudity and some murders and Pamela Stephenson (as Kenny's nerdy assistant Dr Barbara Coyle) has sex with a ghost but this is the sort of film which thinks the height of comedy and shock is to make Vincent Price swear while presiding over a cult ritual.

There are a lot of familiar faces in the film. Don Warrington of Rising Damp, Gareth Hunt of The New Avengers, Cleo Rocos (from Kenny's television show), Graham Stark from the Pink Panther films, and horror icon Vincent Price. Price does his thing in cult robes and I'm sure he had no idea what he was even acting in here. It is rather sad that Bloodbath at the House of Death was the last British horror film that Price ever appeared in. You also get Sheila Steafel, John Fortune, and David Lodge. There is a palpable desperation to some of the performances in the film. You sense that the cast knew this was a stinker as they gamely mug their parts to no avail.

Bloodbath at the House of Death spoofs all manner of films to little effect. Slasher films, An American Werewolf in London, Alien, Invasion of the Body Snatchers, The Wicker Man, E.T. There's a bit of Carry On to the film at times with the innuendo but if you want that you'd be much better off just watching a Carry On film. The film attempts (endlessly) to mine comedy from things like Pamela Stephenson's character having a speech impediment or Kenny's character having a metal leg but none of this is funny. Kenny Everett was a pretty big star in Britain when this film was made and is considered to be something of a genius when it came to radio presenting and radio comedy. His comedy television sketch show was also a very big deal at the time (though unavoidably dated today with its reliance on special effects and scantily clad women).

On the evidence of Bloodbath at the House of Death you'd have to say that Kenny's shtick does not translate into a feature length comedy film. Maybe he was just better in smaller doses. If you take something like The House in Nightmare Park (a film we'll discuss in this book), that works better than Bloodbath at the House of Death as a horror spoof because it is well made in the style of the sort of film it is seeking to parody. The House in Nightmare Park also works better as a horror spoof because you have Frankie Howerd at the heart of it. Howerd has enough presence and talent as a screen comic to take command of The House in Nightmare Park and mask some of its flaws. The same can't be said of Kenny Everett in Bloodbath at the House of Death. You wouldn't even miss Dr Manderville if he vanished from this film whereas you

WOULD miss Frankie Howerd if his Twelvetrees character suddenly vanished from The House in Nightmare Park.

Bloodbath at the House of Death devolves into a series of unfunny comedy sketches (which you could probably show in any order without it making a difference) with terrible editing and wooden performances. By the way, look out for former page 3 girl Debbie Linden as the topless girl at the start. Debbie Linden was in many comedy shows and also stuff like The Wildcats of St Trinians and Bergerac. She sadly died of a drug overdose at the age of thirty-six. Barry Cryer, the writer of this film, has a cameo at the start as a police officer. Sadly, I'm not even joking when I say that Barry gives one of the best performances in the film! And one more thing, before I move on from Bloodbath at the House of Death, at one point the characters in the spooky house have nothing for dinner but then find a pie which has been conveniently left by someone. I wonder if this inspired a similar moment in the amusing Danny Dyer horror film Severance?

BLOODSTREAM (1985)

The prolific zero budget filmmaker Michael J. Murphy churned out a great many films - some of which were lost or never finished. His legacy lives and you can even buy a Michael J. Murphy box-set these days - which is worth a look for the scrappy but amusing horror films which lace the Murphy oeuvre. Bloodstream is one such scrappy horror film. These days anyone can make a zero budget film using their phone but Murphy didn't have that luxury back in 1985. He had to do things the hard way. Bloodstream revolves around a struggling filmmaker named Alistair Bailey (Patrick Oliver) who has just made a cheap horror film called (you guessed it) Bloodstream. The film is screened for William King (Mark Wells) - that is to say he watches it on video in his office. King is a distributor of bargain basement video nasties and sexploitation films. He has a moustache and cigar and is rude to everyone.

Bailey, who is flat broke, has high hopes for Bloodstream but is dismayed when King tells him that the film is a load of old cobblers unworthy of his time. He tells Bailey to sling his hook. Bailey points out that he is owed money and has a contract but King, the crafty and crooked businessman that he is, has this covered and tells Bailey that the small print of the contract (clause 25 to be precise) stipulates that he can terminate their contract at any time should he deem the film to be a load of cobblers. As he has literally just done that, Bailey, in legal terms, doesn't have a leg to stand on. Mr King did not get where is by being nice. That's for sure.

Bailey goes home to his grotty flat to mope and watch horror films. There is a twist because King has swindled him. In reality, King thinks that Bloodstream could be a nice little earner. King distributes the film without telling Bailey - thus keeping the money for himself. However, King's long suffering secretary Nikki (Jacqueline Logan) tells Bailey what has happened and together they devise a grisly horror film themed revenge...

Bloodstream is very rough around the edges (which is obviously to be expected) and the acting is terrible (which is also to be expected). The story was apparently inspired by Michael J. Murphy being ripped off by a distributor himself. Making this film must have been rather cathartic you'd imagine. Bailey dresses up as a masked killer from his horror film and basically murders everyone connected to King - including his wife, mistress, brother-in-law, and daughter. King's dog even buys it too - which I didn't appreciate too much. Keep dogs out of these films please.

What is most fun about Bloodstream is the little clips from horror films we get when Bailey watches videos at home. Some of these are from Murphy's own films. The mash-up of all this weird stuff is not unlike the frazzled style of the V/H/S anthology franchise which is quite popular today. The 'films within a film' gimmick of Bloodstream is by far its biggest trump card and these little clips are an enjoyably mixed bag of horror tropes. Some are amusing, some are hokey, some are gruesome, some are silly. There's even a smidgen of soft-porn thrown into the blender. There's an Exorcist rip-off with green vomit, zombies, a man ripping his face off, gladiator fights, a hunchback, a werewolf, vampires.

My favourite clip by far is where some suave cannibal killer is having dinner with a woman and, when she inquires as to what she is eating, he calmly tells her she is dining on her husband's bottom. Bailey shoots the murders he commits on a camera in order to create the ultimate 'real' horror film. Peeping Tom is obviously the biggest touchstone for Murphy in terms of his concept here. There is a fun amount of gore in Bloodstream and the most graphic death comes when a woman gets a knife down her throat. Having said that though there's a nasty bit in the Exorcist knock-off where the priest ends up with electrodes in his eyes. The basic premise of Bloodstream is fun and while Michael J. Murphy is not Wes Craven and was working here with a budget that wouldn't even stretch to a packet of Wotsits and a can of pop, this film is fun too for the most part.

I'm not entirely convinced there is quite enough story and mayhem here to justify a feature length running time and Bloodstream is not without a few dull stretches but it is fascinating and enjoyable nonetheless to be taken back in time to the world of low-budget British horror filmmaking aimed at the video market during the video nasty era. Murphy seems to have a few points to make about the impact of screen violence but the main subtext of this film seems to be that poverty, getting ripped-off, and frustration turn people bad - not cheap horror films. One criticism I would add in relation to the film is that the incessant synth score in Bloodstream makes it very difficult to pick up all of the dialogue. You do find yourself straining at times to decipher what someone has just said.

There is a bit of a twist at the end of Bloodstream which you will probably see coming. Murphy has fun in the last shot by paying homage to Psycho. Bloodstream is not by any stretch of the imagination a good film. It is badly made and has terrible acting. But it is fun and quite inventive in its own strange way. The melange of strange images becomes quite compelling in the end and you admire the plucky effort of everyone involved. Murphy, before he sadly passed away, did a new version of this in which the dubbing of the actors was improved. Murphy also redubbed the part of the sleazy distributor character himself. Bloodstream is easy to stream these days so worth a look if you are curious. In fact, the last time I checked you could even watch this on YouTube.

BLOODY NEW YEAR (1987)

Bloody New Year (aka Time Warp Terror) was directed by Norman J. Warren and written by Frazer Pearce. Warren is best known for films like Prey and maybe Inseminoid. Bloody New Year, which was the last feature length film Warren made, is fairly obscure by comparison although it has appeared on Talking Pictures quite recently. This film was not a happy experience for Norman J. Warren. He complained that the producer had no interest in horror films and was also unhappy about the musical score (featuring songs by Magnus and Chas Cronk's band Cry No More). If his later interviews are anything to go by, Warren had pretty much disowned Bloody New Year and didn't think too much of it at all.

Anyway, what is the plot of this film? That's a very good question. A group of teenagers (all of whom, in traditional horror film fashion, look a bit long in the tooth to be teenagers) are at the seaside and rescue an American tourist named Carol - who is being pestered by thugs. To escape, the group end up, as you do, taking to a boat and aimlessly drifting out into deep water. The gang run ashore on a place named Grand Island. On the island, which seems devoid of people, they find a hotel. Things become stranger yet because the hotel is empty. Not only that but the hotel seems to be frozen in time. Everything in the hotel is in the style of the 1950s. Despite it being the middle of summer the hotel is full of New year's Eve banners and decorations. Having an empty hotel all to yourself doesn't sound too bad but things quickly go pear shaped for our suspiciously mature looking teenagers. Apparitions, zombies, disembodied voices, snowstorms. They should have just stayed at the seaside and played Out Run in the arcade.

You could probably describe Bloody New Year as something of a missed opportunity if you were being very generous. It feels like Warren just wanted to make a crazy horror film in a spooky location but a horror film with a big concept. A sort of Evil Dead meets The Shining meets The Twilight Zone. The frozen time concept is quite interesting though hardly original. Rod Serling's Twilight Zone would have had this concept done and dusted in twenty-five minutes. Bloody New Year, unlike The Twilight Zone, has ninety-three minutes to fill and plainly struggles to do this. We take a bit too long to reach the spooky hotel section of the story if you ask me. The film that Bloody New Year seems most inspired by is Lucio Fulci's The Beyond. The Beyond, like Bloody New Year, is incoherent and eccentric, but it is better directed, has a better cast, and is more fun to return to and watch again.

The lack of recognisable names in the cast of Bloody New Year is perhaps one explanation for why the acting is hit or miss, well, mainly miss if we are being honest. The only person I recognised was Mark Powley as Rick. Powley played P.C Melvin in 88 episodes of The Bill. Suzy Aitchison, who plays Lesley, is the daughter of June Whitfield and has appeared in many comedy shows. The acting in this film is pretty terrible if truth be told. There is a slapdash and amateurish quality to

Bloody New Year - especially in its early scenes. This is probably not surprising given that it had a minuscule budget of £60,000. The lack of a budget leads to some very poor practical effects at times. The film does perk up when the crazy hotel shenanigans kick in and there are some moments of gore and one or two inventive scenes. The hotel cinema (which is showing Fiend Without a Face) having someone walk through the screen (Purple Rose of Cairo style) to murder a character is quite a nice touch.

Bloody New Year bites off a bit more than it can chew in the end with all the crazy horror stuff at the hotel. It doesn't have the budget, competence, or cast to pull off the rollercoaster sort of horror film it wants to be. While parts of the film are quite diverting there isn't much atmosphere so it rings a bit hollow ultimately. The characters are rather bland too so it is difficult to invest in them very much. One disappointing aspect to the film is that Norman J. Warren had intended it to be much bloodier but had to make it tamer to get a lower certificate. Bloody New Year may have mitigated a few more of its obvious flaws if it had a lot more gore and some more memorable deaths than the ones we get in the film. It is difficult to be too harsh about a film made for sixty grand over three odd weeks but Bloody New Year never quite clicks for me - despite its promising premise.

Bloody New Year is one of those films that you want to like more than you actually do. The shoestring budget is all too apparent and the cast are fairly hopeless. I'm sure this film must have fans though so it might be worth a go if you've never seen it - purely for Norman J. Warren completest purposes. The one thing about the film I did like was the frozen time concept because I love films and television shows where characters are trapped somewhere and whatever they do they can't leave. Bloody New Year was shot in Barry Island and even made some use of the Butlin's camp (which closed in 1996) there. So while this might not be a very good film it did make a small piece of cinema history because it's hard to imagine any other horror films were ever shot at Butlin's Barry Island. By the way, the building used as the hotel in the film is Friar's Point House, Paget Road, Barry Island. The property was first built in 1858 by Francis Crawshay.

THE BRAIN (1962)

The Brain was directed by Freddie Francis and based on Donovan's Brain by Curt Siodmak. The Brain was the third film adaptation of this story (after 1944's The Lady and the Monster and 1953's Donovan's Brain) so this particular type of story (while not approaching Monkey's Paw levels) was already becoming a staple for horror filmmakers. This was actually the first horror film that the great Freddie Francis directed. In the years to come he would direct another twenty-seven billion of them. You could probably call The Brain something of a forgotten film in that few people ever watched it and even those who did probably forgot about it quite quickly. This is one of those films that rarely - if ever - got shown on television. Even if it had been on the telly a lot I don't think The Brain would have built up much of a following among vintage horror fans. If you are looking for lurid brain in a jar capers here you might disappointed. For most of its running time The Brain doesn't feel much like a horror film - despite the well worn concept which underpins the story.

In the film, scientist Dr Peter Corrie (Peter van Eyck) has been conducting experiments on how to keep a brain alive after death. He has an unexpected chance to test this on a human being when wealthy businessman Martin Holt (Jeremy Spenser) is seriously injured in a plane crash. Dr Corrie manages to remove the brain before Holt dies and keeps it in a chemical tank. The brain proves to be a lot more active and lively than he had anticipated. Not only that but Holt's brain begins to exert a hypnotic mental control over Dr Corrie. Holt's brain, with Dr Corrie under his control, seems intent on trying to find if the plane crash was a murder...

This film is unavoidably dated today but it is modestly watchable after a rather dull early section of Dr Corrie and his colleague Dr Shears in the lab. I can't say though that I ever found The Brain to be an especially gripping or interesting film. It seems to have its fans but you wouldn't call this some lost forgotten gemstone in the British horror film landscape. There isn't much scope to the film and most of it plays out in some fairly constrictive interior sets and rooms. This is quite a dreary looking film that doesn't have a huge amount of panache about it. There isn't much in The Brain that lodges in the memory and stands out too much. I suppose, as far as old horror films go, you would probably describe this as something of a potboiler. The same year that The Brain came out saw the release of horror films like the trippy Carnival of Souls and the colourful Tales of Terror so even in 1962 The Brain was veering dangerously towards old hat territory.

Dr Shears is played by Bernard Lee and this film came out the same year that Lee secured his most famous role - that of M in the James Bond franchise. Bernard Lee was pretty good in horror films because he was one of those actors where you could give him the most ridiculous dialogue safe in the knowledge that he would play it straight and bring a modicum of (usually much needed) gravitas to your film. The Brain turns into more of a crime mystery than anything in the end and plays a bit like a middling episode of Alfred Hitchcock Presents. This is not the most exciting film in the world and clearly didn't have much of a budget (look at that plane sequence) but it does at least have a decent sense of atmosphere. How much you enjoy The Brain will probably depend on how much you enjoy old crime/thriller melodramas.

Anne Heywood, already well established by now, is the female lead and the German actor Peter van Eyck brings a committed performance to the film as Dr Corrie. There are a couple of familiar faces in small roles in the film. Bryan Pringle, who I always remember as the miserable pub landlord in the second series of Auf Wiedersehen, Pet, as a dance hall MC and Patsy Rowlands, several years before she became a Carry On regular, in an uncredited part as a woman at a dance. You'll recognise John Junkin in a very small part and also Allan Cuthbertson. Allan Cuthbertson was in many things but his most famous role was that of the posh colonel with a twitch in the Gourmet Night episode of Fawlty Towers.

I think a problem with The Brain is that you go into it expecting more science fiction and horror scenes than you actually get and so you sort of have to adjust and accept this film is not going in that direction of shocks and copious scenes of a brain with electrodes in a goldfish bowl. The thriller it devolves into is not without its rewards but it isn't something that isn't going to captivate an audience very much or have them praising this fairly forgettable film to the rafters. The Brain is probably not something you will feel compelled to return to again but it is a piece of horror history with the Freddie Francis connection. Given that this was his first horror film The Brain is probably worth at least one watch purely for historic horror reasons alone. Just don't expect too much traditional horror though because The Brain is more of a crime mystery than anything.

COLD LIGHT OF DAY (1989)

There have been endless biopics about serial killers in film and on television and countless films that take inspiration from real life killers. The horror genre is naturally something that lends itself to inspiration from grisly real life killers. These serial killer inspired productions run the full spectrum from prime time prestige TV to grubby exploitation or straight to DVD clunkers. Cold Light of Day was directed by Fhiona-Louise -

who was only twenty-one when she made this. I gather she was studying acting at the time. Cold Light of Day began as a short film but was expanded into an eighty minute feature. Cold Light of Day is a 16mm film based on the crimes of the serial killer Dennis Nilsen. This is one of the most obscure British horror films ever made.

Dennis Nilsen was from Aberdeenshire in Scotland and later moved to London. He was in the army catering corps when he was young and always tormented by the fact that he was gay. He was actually a police officer too for a short period in the early 1970s. Nilsen eventually confessed to murdering fifteen men and said he tried to kill others. His spree took place from 1978 to 1983. At the time he was a civil servant and worked in a Job Centre in central London. The victims were usually gay men of no fixed abode. He would often strangle the victims while they were asleep and sometimes drowned them in the bath. There was necrophilia too because that was Nilsen's thing. What made Nilsen so disturbing was the way he came across as completely calm and highly articulate and thoughtful in interviews. If you met him you would have no idea that he was so dangerous.

Dennis Nilsen, once they decomposed, chopped up his victims and stuffed them in the floorboards of his flat. One can only imagine how that place must have smelled. On one occasion he used a patch of communal grass out the back of his building to burn some victims on a bonfire. Nilsen had to throw some tyres onto the bonfire in a desperate attempt to mask the odour of burning flesh and organs. Nilsen would bathe the bodies of his victims in the bath after he had killed them. Dennis Nilsen was captured because a plumbing company was called out to unblock the drain outside his building. Nilsen had been trying to flush body parts and bones down the toilet. Tests on the bones and remains blocking the drain found that they were human and the drainpipe led directly to Nilsen's flat. When the police searched Nilsen's flat they encountered a nightmarish scene. Nilsen had body parts and torsos hidden all over the place. He even had bags containing the heads of some of his victims. Nilsen killed his victims because he was frightened they would leave him. This was more or less the same explanation the American serial killer Jeffrey Dahmer (also a keen necrophile) later gave for his own crimes.

Serial killers are, by their very nature, all odd, but even by the standards of serial killers Dennis Nilsen was pretty weird. A number of notorious serial killers have indulged in necrophilia but Nilsen took this grisly hobby to absurd lengths. Nilsen would put a dead body in a chair next to him and watch television with it. He would talk to dead people as if they were still alive. Nilsen would even sit down with a corpse and have dinner with it. Nilsen did this for about five years before he essentially doomed himself by blocking up his drain with human flesh. If he'd been the villain in an episode of Columbo, Nilsen would have posed no challenge whatsoever to the raincoated detective. Hollywood often depicts serial killers as elusive criminal masterminds who are always two steps ahead of the police. The reality is very different. Many serial killers are of average or below average intelligence and not exactly impossible to catch. Dennis Nilsen was definitely no criminal mastermind. In fact, Nilsen didn't really seem to care whether he would be caught or not. His actions strongly suggest that he wanted to be captured in the end.

When the disturbing and shocking crimes of Nilsen came to light, the police and the media were surprised when they clapped eyes on the man who was responsible for them. This was not a darkly charismatic lunatic or a feral outsider straight out of serial killer central casting. Dennis Nilsen was, well, rather dull. He was a very dour and dry sort of man. When he went on trial, court reporters were astonished by how ordinary Dennis Nilsen looked. They had been expecting a monster but the quiet bespectacled man sitting in court didn't really conform to their expectations. Cold of Light of Day also depicts its main

Nilsen inspired character as a boring and dour man - which in a strange way makes his crimes more chilling. You might have expected Cold Light of Day to be more controversial than it was given its subject matter (and fairly recent proximity to the real case on which it is based) but the film was quickly forgotten. Because this was such a low-budget and amateurish sort of film I suppose it didn't really attract much attention and so slipped under the moral outrage radar.

Cold Light of Day features Bob Flag as Nilsen (called Jordan March in the film though clearly based on Nilsen). The film is a rather grim experience. It shows Nilsen/March strangling people and boiling heads. Nilsen would boil heads on his oven hob so he could strip the flesh and flush it down the toilet. The story of Dennis Nilsen is grim indeed. Bob Flag seems a bit old to play Nilsen (who was only in his thirties when he was captured) but he's not bad in the film. What the film does well is capture that lonely alienated grotty bedsit world which Nilsen inhabited. It was where he found his victims. He would befriend some vulnerable youngster who needed somewhere to crash for the night. The film is a period piece now because much of the London of Dennis Nilsen has been yuppified (or should that be hipster-fied?) since the 1980s (in case you were wondering, Nilsen lived in Muswell Hill).

Cold Light of Day alters some of the facts of the Nilsen case - most saliently in that March commits far less murders in the film than the real Dennis Nilsen. The film does though have the death of March's grandfather as a pivotal moment in his life - which mirrors that of Nilsen. Dennis Nilsen famously said his grandfather was the most important and reliable person in his life and that he never recovered from the death of this relative. His grandfather was a fisherman and had the closest bond with the young Dennis Nilsen of anyone in the family. Grandfather and grandson would take walks together and spent a lot of time in one another's company. The grandfather therefore assumed a mythical sort of role in the story of Dennis Nilsen. He was the only person who could have saved Dennis Nilsen but through his death he ended up unwittingly creating Dennis Nilsen. This is the bare bones thesis put forward by several writers - not least Dennis Nilsen himself. The sight of his dead grandfather left Dennis Nilsen with a sense that death and love were as one and connected. This, according to the thesis, sowed the seeds for the tragic dysfunction and awful path of Dennis Nilsen's later life.

Cold Light of Day is framed around Jordan March being questioned at a police station after his arrest. We then get flashbacks of his crimes and even parts of his childhood. I suspect the film that inspired Cold Light of Day the most is Henry: Portrait of a Serial Killer - which was also shot on 16mm. Cold Light of Day is nowhere near as good as that film but it does have enough merit to dodge accusations of being pure exploitation. Cold Light of Day is about the alienation of life in a big city and the banal nature of evil.

The grotty world it depicts of greasy spoons and dirty flats reeks of loneliness and desperation. It goes without saying though that this film is not an easy watch and not exactly a barrel of laughs. You probably won't be sitting down to watch this on Christmas Day with the family. It is certainly an interesting film but a strange and unpleasant film too so caveat emptor. By the way, look out for Claire King in Cold Light of Day. She later played Kim Tate in the soap opera Emmerdale.

Incidentally, there was a fresh wave of interest in Dennis Nilsen in 2020 when the acclaimed ITV drama Des was broadcast. Former Doctor Who actor David Tennant played Nilsen. ITV received a smattering of complaints about their drama Des but not too many. The drama was fairly restrained and respectful. It didn't feature Nilsen strangling people and chopping up bodies or anything like that (unlike Cold Light of Day - which has the Nilsen inspired lead character stuffing people in floorboards). David Tennant said he was relieved that

Dennis Nilsen died before the drama Des was broadcast because he believed Nilsen would probably have derived some pleasure at being the centre of attention again. The greatest punishment for Nilsen after his arrest was that he was sort of forgotten. He wasn't allowed to be interviewed and later British killers like Harold Shipman and Fred West became more famous than him.

THE COMEBACK (1978)

The Comeback was directed by Pete Walker and written by Michael Sloan and Murray Smith. This film did not have Walker's usual writer David McGillivray - which may partly explain why it seems to be rather forgotten compared to Frightmare and House of Whipcord. Despite some very grisly and shocking moments, this film is more of a slow burn mystery than anything so isn't as cultish as some of Walker's more undiluted horror films. The Comeback revolves around a singer named Nick Cooper (Jack Jones) who is making a (you guessed it) comeback after six years. His manager Webster Jones (David Doyle) has arranged for Nick to stay at a plush rural Surrey mansion to help him concentrate on his music. Nick begins to have strange nightmares and visions and hear strange noises at night. Has he gone crackers or is any of this real? Unknown to Nick, his estranged wife Gail (Holly Palance) was brutally hacked to death by some maniac in a hag mask when she collected some items from the Thames penthouse she shared with him. But who was the killer and what was the motive? And is Nick the next target? Well, stay tuned because all will eventually be revealed.

The Comeback begins in unforgettable fashion when Gail is murdered on the stairs of the penthouse by someone dressed as an old witch. This is a very nasty scene and The Comeback definitely borders on the tasteless the way we keep going back to view the decomposing blood caked face of Gail later in the film. There is another memorable kill which takes place in the basement of the penthouse and you certainly can't accuse The Comeback of lacking blood and gore. These kills aside though much of the film is a mystery whodunnit with most of the story taking place at the mansion. I quite enjoyed the mystery myself but some viewers may find the film a slight chore at times given its run time of one hour and forty minutes. Jack Jones is quite likeable as the lead although it is a bit implausible the way the film depicts him as a former pop sensation with obsessed fans. You might believe that with David Cassidy playing the part maybe but not Jack Jones.

Pamela Stephenson is the love interest Linda Everett - Linda being the secretary of Nick's manager. Pamela Stephenson doesn't have much to do in the film but she's quite good. This is back in the days when she was doing straight acting jobs. She later became an alternative comedian and then a psychologist. There is a scene where Nick and Linda have sex in their car in broad daylight at the seaside by a main road. You'd surely get arrested doing that wouldn't you? David Doyle is very good as Nick's insincere manager Webster (who happens to be a closet transvestite) but the icing on the cake for me is Walker regular Sheila Keith as Doris B - the housekeeper of the mansion. As usual, Keith steals every scene she is in with her deadpan line deliveries. As if that wasn't enough you also get Bill Owen as the gardener Albert B. It's amazing how much younger Bill Owen looks without his Compo costume from Last of the Summer Wine. Sheila Keith and Bill Owen make an enjoyably strange double act in this film.

Richard Johnson pops up as a doctor and look out for V and This Is Spinal Tap star June Chadwick as a nurse. Holly Palance, who plays Gail, retired from acting in the late 1980s. She is probably best known for playing Damien Thorn's nanny in The Omen. Peter Turner, who plays Nick's creepy assistant Harry (Harry wastes no time in offering a detailed review of Linda's breasts once he is alone with her), became friends with

Gloria Grahame as a young actor and later wrote the book on which Film Stars Don't Die in Liverpool was based. For some reason, Harry wears a woolly hat throughout the film. I like to think this is an amusing in-joke related to Compo being in the film - only without his trademark woolly hat. Harry's tight red leather jacket is certainly a sight to behold. Penny Irving, who has a small bit as a singer, was in House of Whipcord. She was also a page 3 girl and (among other things) played a secretary in Are You Being Served?

The house used for the film is Foxwarren Park, at Wisley in Surrey. This is a Victorian country house. The penthouse of Nick in the film is terrifying if you ask me. To get to the penthouse you have to walk through a spooky derelict basement area and then go up in one of those caged service lifts. What a creepy place to live. The Comeback is more conventional than most of Pete Walker's other films but it does keep you guessing. They throw a lot of red herrings at you and then completely pull the rug out at the end. If they removed the blood and gore you could imagine this as an episode of Hammer House of Mystery & Suspense. It wouldn't be nearly as much fun though. The Comeback doesn't stick in the memory for very long and is far from the best film Pete Walker made but it is watchable and perfectly decent for what it is. It is worth watching for Sheila Keith alone.

CORRUPTION (1968)

Corruption was directed by Robert Hartford-Davis. The film stars Peter Cushing as Sir John Rowan, a renowned surgeon, and Sue Lloyd as Lynn Nolan, his much younger fiancee. Lynn works as a fashion model and while being photographed at some Swinging Sixties style party, Rowan, increasingly irritated by the risqué nature of the photographs being taken of Lynn, gets into a fight with a photographer. I can't say I blame Dr Rowan here. The people at the party are insufferable and treat him like some doddery old fossil. In the resulting chaos caused by this fracas, a lamp falls on Lynn and badly disfigures her face - ruining her looks. She feels as if her life is ruined but Rowan devises a way to restore her looks using a glandular extract from the glands of corpses. There is only one problem though - and it's a big problem at that. The effect is only temporary. Dr Rowan needs fresh corpses from time to time. Rowan will have to resort to murder on a fairly regular basis if he wants to maintain Lynn's looks.

This is a fairly obscure British horror film but it is a lot fun. It's probably the closest we ever got to seeing Peter Cushing in a British style Grindhouse exploitation film. Corruption is a lot sleazier and violent than the Amicus and Hammer films and Cushing's character, who is refined and gentle at the start, has to become a crazed serial killer because he will literally do anything to please his much younger girlfriend. It's a story of obsession. They say there's no fool like an old fool and that's definitely the case with Dr Rowan. He will do anything for Lynn - even commit murder. Lynn is as much the villain of the piece as Rowan.

Rowan becomes an unhinged lunatic but he is at least aware that what he is doing is wrong. In the end he becomes reluctant to kill but if he doesn't he will lose Lynn. He can't win whatever he does. There is a decent amount of tension in the film and the scene where Rowan decides to murder a prostitute is very compelling. At times the film plays a bit like that Hitchcock film Frenzy (though Corruption is obviously not as polished and inventive as Frenzy). The start of the film is interesting because you have this clash of generations. Dr Rowan is completely out of his element at the madcap Swinging Sixties party and seems like he's just wandered in from another century.

The film has some nice beach scenes (shot on location at Hope Gap Beach in Seaford, East Sussex) near the end and it is compelling when Rowan and Lynn take in a young girl named Terry (Wendy Varnals) as a potential victim. The home invasion stuff at the end feels somewhat silly and generic and the ending might feel a cop-out to some but, generally, this film is bizarre enough to be very entertaining and it is something a bit different from all the Gothic and period British horror films which abounded in this era. Corruption feels trashier and more daring than the other British horror films being produced at this time and these qualities make it very watchable today. You wouldn't pretend this was an accomplished or amazing film but out of the three Robert Hartford-Davis films which feature in this book I'd say that Corruption is the most fun.

By the way, there are some very familiar faces with small roles in this film. Anthony Booth (the 'Scouse git' from Alf Garnett) is the annoying smug photographer at the party and this sequence also features the legendary Vanessa Howard as a ditsy young woman. As ever, Howard steals the scenes she is in. David Lodge, Kate O'Mara, and Bill Murray also feature in the film. Sue Lloyd was in all manner of stuff in her career but probably became best known for her role as Barbara Hunter in the motel themed midlands soap opera Crossroads. Corruption may not be as well-known as other films of the era but has gained a modest cult following over the years for its unique blend of crazy Frankenstein style horror and serial killer crime elements. The film features fairly graphic scenes of violence and gore for the time (though they've obviously been tamed by the passage of time), characteristic of the exploitation films of the late 1960s. It is certainly fun to see Cushing in a slightly different type of horror film. Corruption is not what you would describe as a lost classic but it is a lot of fun and very watchable.

CRAZE (1974)

Craze was directed by Freddie Francis and based on the book

The Infernal Idol by Henry Seymour. In the film Jack Palance plays Neal Mottram, an antiques shop owner and dealer. It is at this point though that any comparisons with Lovejoy must come to an end. Mottram is not a charming poodle haired rogue in a leather jacket who becomes involved in comical mysteries in East Anglia. Mottram is into witchcraft and occultism. He worships a statue of Chuku in his shop basement and offers up regular sacrifices to the idol by murdering women - convinced that Chuku rewards him with wealth, protection, and good luck in return. However, the police soon start to get a trifle suspicious about Mottram and start sticking their nose into his affairs. Can he stay one step ahead of them while still offering grisly sacrifices to Chuku? One thing is certain. This definitely never happened to Ian McShane and Tinker.

Craze begins with a camp occult ceremony in Mottram's basement and then he commits a murder - though this first one is more of an accident. With the bills piling up around his ears (join the club Mr Mottram) and the rent overdue, Mottram finds some gold coins in a drawer. He decides that the coins were a reward from Chuku for the sacrifice of the woman and so murder now becomes his main hobby. You think this is basically going to be formula for the whole film - Mottram luring women to his basement to murder them. Craze doesn't do this though and opens up as a film with Mottram going on the road to murder his wealthy aunt (played by Edith Evans) for the inheritance. In order to give himself an alibi he visits an old flame in the form of guesthouse owner Dolly (Diana Dors). Mottram gets Dolly drunk on cherry brandy he has laced with sedatives so that she thinks they spent the night together when in fact he was out trying to make sure his aunt kicked the bucket.

There's certainly a pleasant novelty to watching the larger than life Jack Palance wandering around these charmingly mundane English locations (the film was made in and around Shepperton I believe). While some reviews seem to find the police investigation parts of this film slightly wearing I quite liked them myself. It helps a lot that you have Michael Jayston as Wall, the main copper on Mottram's tail. Wall doesn't like Mottram at all and thinks this antiques shop rascal's alibis are too smooth to be credible. You also get Trevor Howard as the police chief and Percy Herbert as Detective Russet. With actors of this calbre in the film the police stuff is all very watchable. I rather enjoyed the game of cat and mouse between Jayston and Palance in the film. Admittedly, some of these actors are slumming it here - when Trevor Howard passed away the newspapers most likely didn't go 'CRAZE STAR DIES' in their obituary headlines.

It's fun to see Diana Dors in the film as the guesthouse woman who Palance pretends to care about merely to have an alibi. By this stage of her career Dors was typecast as nagging wives, mysterious grannies, and flirtatious older women who had seen better days. Jayston's police officer Wall becomes suspicious of Mottram's alibi of sleeping with the Dors character Dolly because he doesn't think the vain and fastidious Mottram would be interested in someone like that. Jayston, in reference to the Dors character, says something along the lines of 'you wouldn't want to dock in that port'. It's a curious and rather cruel line for them to put in the film as it is basically saying that Diana Dors - once Britain's version of Marilyn Monroe - is now an old boiler. You'd like to think they got Diana's permission to include the line. Maybe she just took as a reference to her character and didn't take it personally.

You wouldn't say this was the best Jack Palance performance by a long shot but he's effective as the sleazy Mottram and I like the way his character seems to enjoy matching wits with the police. Palance only really goes bonkers at the end so he's quite restrained overall. Martin Potter plays Ronnie, the young man who lives with Mottram and works as his assistant. It seems to heavily implied these two are a gay couple - which might explain why Palance seems to be faintly disgusted when he has to seduce a woman. Suzy Kendall is amusing as an orange wigged prostitute and Mottram victim who has more toys than Ann Summers in her cupboard. If anyone steals this film though it is Hugh Griffith as the solicitor. The eyebrows of Griffith are also great scene stealers. By the way, look out for David Warbeck as one of the plain clothes coppers near the end.

Craze has some death and gore but it is fairly tame compared to many other horror films of the 1970s. There are a couple of funny scenes where characters go into nightclubs or disco bars. I always find it amusing how in real life if you went in a real nightclub it would probably be full of eighteen year-olds and yet in old films nightclubs and discos seem to be full of middle-aged people wearing blazers. I quite enjoyed Craze on the whole but I wouldn't pretend this is an especially accomplished or memorable film. The end is disappointingly predictable too. The cast alone though makes Craze worth at least one watch.

CURSE OF THE FLY (1965)

Curse of the Fly was directed by Don Sharp and written by Harry Spalding. This is the third film in the trilogy - following on from The Fly and Return of the Fly. Don't look for much continuity between this film and the other two Fly films though because there isn't a lot to connect them together. You just have to treat this film as its own thing with only vague connections to the other two. Curse of the Fly is a British film and was made in England to take advantage of the Eady Levy subsidy. Curse of the Fly (which is in black and white) is set in Quebec and begins with quite an arresting sequence. A woman in her underwear escapes through a window and runs down a country lane.

The woman turns out to be Patricia Stanley (Carole Gray). A passing motorist named Martin Delambre (George Baker) notices the woman and he gives her his jumper to wear and a lift. He then takes her to a hotel and before you know it they are married. It turns out that Patricia escaped from a mental institution. As we soon find out though, compared to the nutty Delambre family she's the picture of sanity. The names and ages of the Delambre family members in this film contradict the previous two Fly films so it is best not to think about that stuff too much and just take this film on its own terms.

Curse of the Fly was a very obscure film for a while and probably still is. Many people who enjoy the first two films (especially the first one) tend to be disappointed by Curse of the Fly - mostly for one specific reason. That reason is the lack of fly/human hybrid capers. Fly/human hybrid capers are not merely in short supply in this film but completely absent. There is not a single scene in this film where a character ends up with a giant fly's head and I suppose for some fans of this franchise that is unavoidably going to be a disappointment. You could venture that Curse of the Fly is sort of like the Halloween III (or even Halloween Ends) of the Fly series. It just wanted to do something different and not repeat the same formula again. Whether or not this approach worked is certainly debatable though.

It transpires that in their private mansion in the countryside, the Delambre family are still engaged in the teleportation experiments we saw in the first two films - and which led to the pesky fly/human hybrid palaver. As there is no fly/human hybrid palaver in this third film it becomes instead a sort of Gothic science fiction horror yarn. A number of 'mutants' ended up disfigured thanks to the experiments and are shoved away in the stables by the Delambre family. The disfigured mutants include Martin's wife - who he neglected to tell Patricia about. Martin is therefore not just a mad scientist but also a bigamist.

Brian Donlevy is Martin's father Henri Delambre in the film and, like George Baker (who is plainly struggling trying to do a

Canadian accent), gives a rather dry and dour performance. This third film in the Fly franchise desperately misses Vincent Price. There are a couple of oriental assistants working for the Delambre family named Tai and Wan - which is plainly a joke. Tai is played by (no surprise here) the Lancashire born and Chinese raised Burt Kwouk. However, the other assistant, Wan, is played by the Welsh actress Yvette Rees with her eyes turned up and a risible foreign accent. You definitely couldn't that in a film today.

The hokey laboratory scenes with clunky machines and plenty of dials to press are not without charm and Curse of the Fly does have its moments. There is an effective sequence where Patricia is woken by someone playing the piano downstairs and when she investigates it turns out to Martin's disfigured wife Judith (Mary Manson). Judith is the Mrs Rochester in the attic - or the stables in this case. The most chilling moment in the film comes when the Delambre deliberately teleport two men together to their teleportation pod in London - knowing full well the two men will be fused together and perish. This is an unexpected moment of body horror which was probably quite shocking in 1965 to the six people who actually watched this film when it was released. The basic plot of the film is that the police are closing in on the Delambre family so the Delambres are trying to cover their tracks and get rid of any loose ends.

Curse of the Fly is nowhere near as much fun as the first two Fly films but, taken for what it is, it certainly isn't terrible. The film has plenty of atmosphere and a couple of memorable moments. The music is good and the increasingly downbeat nature of the film sort of works to its advantage. The concept is quite interesting in that the Delambre family are toiling away in secret trying to perfect this amazing technology but never quite succeeding in that aim - which leads only to trouble and tragedy. By the way, despite the lack of fly themed horror antics in this film, the famous line "Help me! Help me!" is muttered at one point. Curse of the Fly is certainly watchable but the weak dialogue and dull cast (save perhaps for Carole Gray) are handicaps the film is always having to battle against. If you like the first two films this is worth a look for completist purposes but just don't expect any fly shenanigans.

DAEMON (1985)

Daemon was written and directed by Colin Finbow. This was a production by the Children's Film Unit. The CFU was a registered educational charity and offered children the chance to participate in the production of films. Daemon is a kids horror film and concerns young Nick (Arnaud Morell) - who is left in the care of his two sisters and an au pair while his parents are away. Nick begins to notice strange messages on his (amusingly antiquated) computer and also develops blisters on his feet and cuts on his legs. He has dreams of fire and being burned. His friends think he is possessed by a demon and want to drive a stake through his heart. Charming. Can anyone solve the strange mystery of what is afflicting Nick?

Daemon is, as you might expect from a CFU film, somewhat rough around the edges and amateurish. It feels a bit like watching a short film which has been stretched into a longer feature. The child actors in this film are atrocious (a glance at IMDB shows that only a few of the kids had any acting credits beyond this film) - especially the two sisters of Nick who, for reasons which escape me at this precise moment, have orange and blue curly mops of hair respectively. It is obviously very unsporting and unfair of me though to aim any barbs at the acting because these kids were not professionals. Child acting is something that has come a long way in recent years. In the past child actors were often jarringly wooden but these days kids in films and television productions are usually expected to be as polished as the rest of the cast.

One thing I do like about this film though is that the kids are real little kids and the same ages as their characters. If this was a studio film with a budget they'd probably have some hulking twenty-four year-old playing Nick. There are some professional actors in the cast who, unavoidably, stand head and shoulders above these plucky novice child actors. Bert Parnaby is very good as their teacher Mr Crabb. Mr Crabb is found of the occult and dispenses some of this lore in his class. Parnaby was in loads of stuff like Lovejoy, Last of the Summer Wine, The Black Adder, and so on. Mr Crabb, who is the RE (religious education) teacher, seems unusually interested in demons and is easily distracted by the crafty kids. So rather than enduring some boring RE lesson they just get him to talk about witchcraft or something.

Susannah York, who was a patron of the CFU, also adds a much needed shot of gravitas and class to the film as a psychiatrist who talks to Nick. Daemon, as a film for children, obviously isn't The Exorcist but it does have a few creepy POV shots and some of Nick's dreams would be a bit scary for kids to watch I'd imagine. The music score, which seems to riff on a few old classics like Halloween, is fairly enjoyable too. Although the conclusion of this film (which I won't give away) is very derivative it is quite good fun and I did enjoy the cockney child character who turns up at the end. He stole the show for me as far as the kids in this film go. I was disappointed though that it didn't turn out to be a very young Danny Dyer. That would have been fantastic.

Daemon has some themes about loneliness and alienation and perhaps a theme too about Nick realising that kids in the past had it a lot worse than he does. One thing that is fun about Daemon is when the children talk about horror films in class and muse on films like The Omen. Horror films would have been a fairly topical issue in 1985 given the video nasty hysteria of 1984. Daemon is no great shakes, even as a film aimed at children, but it is a likeable effort and its status now as a period piece does make it quite good fun. It is enjoyable to get this little time capsule of a school, youngsters, and houses in 1985. Nick has Doctor Who posters and a Mickey Mouse phone by the looks of it. By the way, in case you were wondering, Nick's computer is (according to my research) apparently an Apple Macintosh.

DARK PLACES (1973)

Dark Places was directed by Don Sharp and written by Ed Brennan and Joseph Van Winkle. This film is not very well known - despite generally being as competent as some of the Amicus and Hammer films being made around this time. There were, I gather, problems with the release of this film - which may explain why it never became very well known. I can't remember ever encountering Dark Places on television. Anyway, the plot concerns the death of a man named Andrew Marr. Marr dies and leaves his spooky country mansion to his friend Edward Foster (Robert Hardy). Foster decides to live in the mansion - despite the stories of it being haunted and a cursed place. Three people who take a very keen interest in Mr Foster are the late Mr Marr's physician Dr Mandeville (Christopher Lee), Mandeville's sister Sarah (Joan Collins), and Mr Marr's solicitor Prescott (Herbert Lom).

What the Mandeville siblings and Mr Prescott all know is that Mr Marr left two suitcases full of money (£200,000) somewhere in the mansion. They are desperate to get their mitts on that money and Edward Foster living there is a complication. Foster is aware of the money too - which is why he chooses to move into this roomy but ramshackle abode. Mr Foster has troubles of his own because he's beginning to have flashbacks related to the former occupant of the house. These flashbacks are revealing but they do threaten Foster's sanity...

On the whole, Dark Places is an enjoyable daft thriller with some horror tropes thrown in for good measure. Early on there are a few too many scenes for my liking of Robert Hardy exploring the mansion and being spooked by strange noises and voices. Just as this is beginning to become tiresome though the film perks up considerably thanks to Joan Collins as Sarah. Joan has a (rather unconvincing) wig which actually anticipates Alexis Carrington and she is in full on smirking gold digger mode - the vamp meter turned up to eleven. Sarah seduces Edward and reports back to her prissy brother - who is disgusted by Sarah in the manner of Victorian Dad from Viz but in cahoots all the same because he wants that money. There's a weird moment where Sarah tells Dr Mandeville he must wish she wasn't his sister sometimes. Blimey.

We see the flashbacks Edward is having about Mr Marr in the form of scenes from the past - where Robert Hardy is playing Marr too. Marr is a more stern and old-fashioned chap than Foster and you get the impression that Robert Hardy is in his comfort zone a lot more playing a stern old fashioned chap than he is saucily romping with Joan Collins. What makes this film enjoyable as much as anything is that it revolves around this small cast of old pros who all work well together. Herbert Lom is really good fun too as the solicitor for the estate who seems like a really nice man but in reality is after that money too. I don't think Christopher Lee is too stretched here by playing a posh doctor up to no good but his scenes with Joan Collins give us a fine double act we never knew we needed.

The flashback scenes include a young Jane Birkin as Alta - the governess Marr planned to leave his wife for. Marr's neurotic wife is played by Jean Marsh so there are familiar faces everywhere you look in this film. Jean Marsh has an amusingly hammy scene where she goes stark raving bonkers while setting the dinner table. One problem with the flashback segments and the way they run parallel to the main story is that you have a fairly good idea where this is all heading so there aren't really any huge surprises at the end (although, having said that, the end is slightly darker than you expect). The spooky house stuff is also, as we have noted, a trifle rote to say the least.

A scene where Foster is attacked by bats doesn't really work because it is patently obvious they are just rubber bats on pieces of string. I don't think we are supposed to be taking this film very seriously though so maybe we can let the inadequacies of the bat capers slide. There isn't much blood and mayhem in the film but you do get a strangulation and a (fairly bloodless) pickaxe murder. Foster goes increasingly doolally in the house but Robert Hardy is not the most frightening or dangerous maniac ever put on film. While the haunted house antics are derivative the film does work as a thriller with the characters all after the stashed money. Dr Mandeville and Sarah think they can play Foster for a mug so we are eager for them to get their comeuppance.

Dark Places is not some undiscovered classic but it is decent fun and worth the price of admission for Joan Collins alone. The story is probably too overstuffed for its own good in the end but some of the plotting is quite clever and it did keep me entertained until the end. Dark Places was shot in and around Uxbridge and Foster's house was an abandoned asylum in real life. You can tell the film must have been shot in winter because it looks parky and the characters are wrapped up in coats and jumpers. This film got terrible reviews when it came out and doesn't seem to be fondly remembered by too many people but I quite enjoyed it myself. If you are expecting a pure horror film though you may be disappointed by the relatively tame and bloodless nature of Dark Places.

DEAD END (1980)

Dead End is a horror short film written and directed by Alan Birkinshaw. Birkinshaw is best known for the infamous Killer's Moon (a film we will discuss later in this book). Dead End is about twenty-five minutes long and was considered a lost film for a while but was recently cleaned up and put on YouTube. It was scanned from a rare 35mm print by the channel RecordCouncil - so hats off to that YouTuber for giving us a chance to see this rare piece of British horror history for ourselves. Oddly, this short horror film was shown before screenings of Smokey and the Bandit II. What a bizarre double bill!

The premise of Dead End is amazingly simple and very effective. A young woman named Mary (Belinda Mayne - future star of Don't Open Till Christmas, a film we will also discuss shortly) parks her car in an empty multi-story car park that is about to close because she has a few things she needs from the supermarket. She ends up trapped in the car park and menaced by an unseen prowler who seems intent on running her down. Mary has been getting threatening phone calls from a mysterious man so this is plainly no coincidence.

Aided by the brief running time, Dead End is lean and tense in a way that Killer's Moon often wasn't. The restoration of this film has made it look very blue but the spooky car park makes a good constrictive location and Belinda Mayne is a great horror heroine. The film begins with her playing tennis and her opponent is none other than Jenny Seagrove (in her acting debut). So we get Belinda Mayne in a tennis outfit and then cut to her taking a bath at home. Suffice to say, Birkinshaw is not shy when it comes to taking advantage of the sex appeal of his leading lady.

I found the scenes of Mary shopping endlessly fascinating because we get to see what a supermarket looked like in 1980. Much the same as a supermarket today if truth be told. Mary is rather disappointed to learn though that they've run out of courgettes - which are literally the last thing I'd be disappointed to find the supermarket had run out of. Horrible things if you ask me. This short film is full of surprises and one such surprise comes next when Mary pays for her goods. The check out girl on the till is played by none other than Tracy Hyde - co-star of the cult film Melody with Mark Lester. It looks like Tracy was struggling to find acting jobs by 1980. It can be a tough old racket. Someone has slipped a knife in Mary's basket. This supermarket sequence is somewhat reminiscent the supermarket scene in Schizo - which is yet another film we'll get around to in this book.

When she goes back to her car, Mary finds that her dog Mish is missing and then becomes aware that someone else is in the car park and stalking her - well driving after her while she's on foot. There's an effective score and the darkness of the location works to the advantage of the film. You can imagine Dead End working very nicely in an anthology television show. The bare bones simplicity of the premise works to its advantage. The conclusion of Dead End is rather amusing today because the prowler is revealed to be Alan Ford - who is most associated these days for his funny turns as a cockney gangster in Armando Iannucci's comedy shows.

Dead End is a fascinating little slice of obscure British horror history and great fun. Given that it is only twenty-five minutes long too you have no excuses for not sampling it for yourself.

DEVIL DOLL (1964)

Devil Doll was directed and produced by Lindsay Shonteff. In the film, a stage magician and hypnotist named The Great Vorelli (Bryant Haliday) performs to packed houses with his ventriloquist's dummy Hugo. A reporter named Mark English (William Sylvester) is assigned to write a story about Vorelli and is especially curious to find out how the magician manages to have his dummy Hugo walk around the stage as if it is a real person. English has his girlfriend Marianne (Yvonne Romain) tag along and this proves to be a mistake as

Vorelli has designs on her and as a hypnotist is dangerous indeed when it comes to women. It transpires that Vorelli is a man with a lot of secrets. Not only that but he's a dodgy character too with a very wonky moral compass...

Devil Doll is unavoidably indebted to the Michael Redgrave segment in the 1945 British compendium horror film Dead of Night. The dummy even has the same name - Hugo. I think an obvious problem facing Devil Doll is that it has a premise which could have been done more effectively in half the time. The segment in Dead of Night is pretty short and you've had great half-hour anthology episodes mining a similar sort of theme - like The Twilight Zone episode The Dummy and the Alfred Hitchcock Presents episode The Glass Eye. Devil Doll is over eighty minutes long and struggles at times to fill the space. You probably could have done this as a half-hour anthology episode and it would have been more to the point with all of the filler material trimmed off.

I can never quite decide if the performance of Bryant Haliday as Vorelli in this film is one-note prime teak or inspired. He maintains the same tone for practically the entire film. I suppose it sort of works because this is an unemotional sort of man who has to maintain a lot of mental discipline to perform his stage act. I'm not entirely convinced by that fake looking beard though. Devil Doll is suitably creepy at times and has some memorable moments. There's a Twilight Zone style twist in the tale (which is utterly ludicrous but this is an old horror film and not to be taken too seriously) and it is also enjoyably weird when Hugo walks around on the stage unaided. I gather that they did this by putting a 4'2 woman inside the dummy. Anyway, the effect is creepy and Hugo, like most ventriloquist's dummies, is a spooky little blighter.

Although the old 'ventriloquist's dummy battles the ventriloquist for control' plot has been done a million times, Devil Doll has enough variations on this theme to just about justify its existence and feel like something slightly different. At the very least it does approach the stock nutty ventriloquist story from a few different weird angles. The fact that Vorelli is more of a hypnotist than a ventriloquist is a case in point. There's quite a fun scene at the start where Vorelli hypnotises Marianne into dancing the twist. Devil Doll is not the most exciting or well produced horror film you'll ever watch and does have some dull stretches but there's quite a good atmosphere and the stage stuff is interesting and generally well done.

For what it is, Devil Doll is certainly not bad. The only problems are the fact that you've seen this type of story done better elsewhere and in less than half the time too. There isn't really any compelling reason why this story had to be told in an eighty minute feature length format. On the whole though this is certainly watchable and Yvonne Romain is a standout as Marianne. The main problem with the film is the pacing and inconsistent story in that you get great chilling moments spliced with fairly boring stretches. With better pacing and a few more chills this could have been a pretty good film but even as it is Devil Doll is by no means a bad film at all.

DOCTOR BLOOD'S COFFIN (1961)

Doctor Blood's Coffin was directed by Sidney J. Furie. The film was based on a short story set in the United States. The story is changed in the film and takes place in Cornwall. The plot has strange things happening in a Cornish village. People are disappearing. Back at the village after some time away is Dr Peter Blood (Kieron Moore). Peter's father Robert (Ian Hunter) is the village doctor. It turns out that Peter knows a lot more about the strange goings on in the village than he is willing to admit. He is determined to prove that science can defeat death and has been kidnapping test subjects to test out his theory. His father's nurse Linda (Hazel Court) becomes friendly with Peter. Will she uncover the dastardly secret he is hiding?

Despite its B movie title and subject matter, Doctor Blood's Coffin is surprisingly straight faced and conventional for most of its running time. The pacing is slow and it doesn't go in for cheap shocks or campiness. The authentic location work in Cornwall adds to the atmosphere and the Irish actor Kieron Moore is quite good in the lead role as Dr Blood. This film is basically a mad scientist caper but Moore's performance is not as bonkers as you might expect considering he is playing a mad scientist horror villain. He does have his moments though. Moore is not the most charismatic actor in the world but he's not bad. I'd imagine that if this film was made a decade later they'd probably have got someone like Ralph Bates to play Dr Blood. Able support is on hand from Hazel Court - who built up an impressive CV of cult film and television, everything from Hammer to The Twilight Zone.

Doctor Blood's Coffin is not the most exciting film in the world and is longer than it probably needed to be but it's a decent chiller with some good actors. The fact that the film takes its time and assumes you have an attention span is something of a novelty from a modern vantage point. The plot in this film is quite similar to that of Re-Animator in that you have a scientist convinced he can bring people back to life but having to do this on the sly. The difference here is that Dr Blood is kidnapping people he considers 'worthless' and not worthy of life. He wants to replace them with more 'worthy' people. Blood is playing God and like all mad scientists in all mad scientist films who play God it probably isn't going to turn out too well for him in the end.

Doctor Blood's Coffin is often cited as the first colour horror film to feature a zombie in the modern horror film sense of a zombie. That is to say a pasty ghoul trying to mindlessly claw you into its clutches. The zombie in this film genuinely does anticipate everything that would follow - from Plague of the Zombies to Night of the Living Dead and so on. The problem is that you only get about two minutes of zombie action in Doctor Blood's Coffin. If you go into this film expecting zombies galore you are going to be disappointed. The zombie make-up is excellent and detailed when it finally arrives. You can see they put a lot of effort into the zombie for the big climax.

Doctor Blood's Coffin was considered to be quite a shocking film when it came out and got an X-certificate. These days Doctor Blood's Coffin seems remarkably tame but the last part of the film is certainly creepy and well done. There is a smidge of gore here and there. The Cornish locations are probably the main star of the film and nicely photographed. There are cave and mine locations too. The interiors of the film were shot in a London studio. The sets are very good in these scenes. I don't think

Doctor Blood's Coffin is going to knock anyone's socks off these days and it isn't as much fun as the Hammer films but this certainly isn't a bad film at all. Doctor Blood's Coffin is unavoidably dated but with its depiction of a modern film zombie it does have its own special spot in horror history.

DOMINIQUE (1979)

After end of Amicus Productions, Milton Subotsky's new company Sword & Sorcery Productions made Dominique - a 1979 horror thriller directed by Michael Anderson. The film is based on the 1948 short story What Beckoning Ghost by Harold Lawlor. Dominique stars Cliff Robertson as a businessman named David Ballard. Ballard lives in England with his rich wife Dominique (Jean Simmons). It is Dominique who has inherited wealth. She is the one keeps his business afloat and pays the bills in this family. Ballard has been playing mean tricks on Dominique though in order to make her go insane. He wants to get rid of his wife so he can get his greedy paws on her money.

Ballard makes Dominique think the house is haunted and employs various tricks to make her began to question her increasingly frazzled grip on sanity. The diabolical scheme works in the end. Dominique commits suicide by hanging herself in the conservatory and Ballard is happy because he now has her money. But not so fast. She then begins to apparently haunt him from the grave and now Ballard is the one who has his sanity under question...

Dominique is basically like watching a mildly interesting fifteen minute segment of Rod Serling's Night Gallery but stretched out into a feature length film. There is an awful lot of padding in this picture. We get endless shots of Cliff Robertson looking thoughtful or walking up and down the stairs. This must have been one of the easiest jobs of Robertson's career. He barely speaks in much of the film. There weren't too many lines for him to learn on the plane. The casting of the usually terrific Robertson is rather wasted. He often looks as if he hasn't the faintest idea what he is even acting in.

There are a raft of scenes in the story which play out with hardly any dialogue in order to (presumably) stretch out the running length. This all gives the film a slow burn quality that does rather tend to test your patience in the end. The actual look and atmosphere of the film is not unlike watching an episode of Hammer House of Mystery & Suspense, an anthology show that made a stock in trade of these types of murder/revenge/madness sort of stories. Most of the action in Dominique is confined to the big house of Ballard and it is shot to look as shadowy and mysterious as possible. So shadowy in fact you can't barely see what is going on half the time!

Although the story is highly derivative (you can't help feeling as if you've seen this sort of 'revenge from beyond the grave' plot done millions of times in horror and thriller films and television shows), the direction is competent and there are a slew of familiar faces in the cast. You get Simon Ward in a plum role as Ballard's streetwise young chauffeur, plus Ron Moody, Michael Jayston, Jenny Agutter, Judy Geeson, Leslie Dwyer (aka the miserable Punch and Judy man from Hi-de-Hi!), David Tomlinson (from Mary Poppins and Bedknobs & Broomsticks), and Jack Warner. They really managed to get a load of famous actors crammed into this film. Not all of them have a lot to do but there are many familiar faces who are fun to spot.

One obvious criticism of Dominique is that the twist is quite easy to predict. It's not that difficult from a very early stage in the film to work out what is really going on. It's a common problem with thrillers like this. It's hard to come up with a twist sometimes that no one saw coming. Despite some interesting flourishes, Dominique is weakened by the predictable ending and a story that doesn't really justify the 100 minute running time. Dominique has the sort of plot that Tales from the Unexpected would have done better only in twenty-five minutes. If you like slow burn mysteries though you might get some enjoyment out of this - for the cast if nothing else.

DON'T OPEN TILL CHRISTMAS (1984)

Don't Open Till Christmas was directed by Edward Purdom - who is also the lead actor. Well, he was mostly the director and lead actor. He apparently left the film a few times - leaving them to fend for themselves and rewrite the script but he did come back in the end. The end result was a production nightmare but then it didn't matter too much because this was a micro budget forgotten British slasher film and not Schindler's List. Alan Birkinshaw had a hand in the script of Don't Open Till Christmas. The film was produced by Dick Randall - a prolific low-budget exploitation film figure.

There are a lot of Christmas horror films but few are as nasty and strange as this one. Don't Open Till Christmas is definitely not some lost gem in the British horror landscape but it is actually quite good fun if you approach it in the right frame of mind. The plot of the film has a serial killer murdering anyone he stumbles across who is dressed as Father Christmas. So, if you are a Father Christmas impersonator or have merely donned a Santa suit to go to a fancy dress party then this killer will target you. There is an obvious way to avoid being attacked by this killer. Don't dress as Father Christmas! Anyway, let's not look for too much logic and simply try to get into the (not very festive in this specific case) spirit of things.

Chief Inspector Ian Harris (Edward Purdom) and his assistant Detective Sergeant Powell (Mark Jones) are in charge of the Santa killer investigation. I love the way the film doesn't have the money to depict a police station so they just have Harris and Powell conducting all police business in a tiny room with a giant map of London tacked to the wall behind them! Dragged into this affair is Kate (Belinda Mayne), whose father was killed at a party while dressed as Santa, and her boyfriend Cliff (Gerry Sundquist). Cliff becomes a suspect in the case. Further complicating matters is a reporter named Giles Harrison (Alan Lake). Giles seems very interested in this case and appears to be suggesting that Chief Inspector Harris is hiding a few secrets.

The identity of the killer probably won't come as a huge surprise (you'll work it out fairly soon) but this bargain basement slasher is strangely watchable with a very scuzzy early eighties atmosphere. The most memorable thing about this film are the kills and gore. A man gets a spear in the mouth, someone is memorably (and painfully) attacked at some urinals, there is a machete to the face, stabbings aplenty and so on. Oh, and one Father Christmas has his face burned off. Lovely. If you want blood and slasher carnage then this film will deliver that. There's quite a good sequence at the London

Dungeon and the POV opening shot, though highly derivative in horror films even by 1984, is creepy.

I quite like the part where the police decide to dress some officers as Father Christmas to try and flush the killer out at a market - this plan going about as well as you might expect in a slasher film. Don't Open Till Christmas is laughably cheap and doesn't stand up to any scrutiny but at under ninety minutes it never really threatens to outstay its welcome too much. Edward Purdom, a sort of Tesco Value Richard Johnson, is not bad as the police inspector although you can detect at times that Purdom would rather be doing anything but appear in this film. Belinda Mayne (who we discussed in Dead End) was no stranger to zero budget horror nonsense because a few years before this she was in Ciro Ippolito's cheekily titled Alien 2: On Earth.

Sadly, the cast of this film includes some actors who befell tragic fates. Alan Lake committed suicide before Don't Open Till Christmas came out because he was so depressed at the death of his wife Diana Dors. Gerry Sundquist, who plays Cliff, also committed suicide (in 1993) by throwing himself in front of a train in southwest London. Sundquist, who was once the boyfriend of Nastassja Kinski, was a recovering heroin addict. His last acting job was in an episode of The Bill. There are a couple of very familiar faces in the film in very small parts too. Kevin Lloyd, Tosh Lines from The Bill no less, plays a friend of Cliff and Caroline Munro has a cameo as herself performing a (truly atrocious) song.

Don't Open Till Christmas is often quite inept in an Acorn Antiques sort of way at times and clearly had a non-existent budget but it is good for a few laughs. There are rubbish eighties punks, Soho peep shows, plenty of outdoor location work, and a commendable determination to be as over the top as possible with the kills. By any technical criteria this is a terrible film but it is worth watching at least once. As far as

Christmas horror films go, Don't Open Till Christmas is definitely no Black Christmas but it is more fun than the infamous American slasher Silent Night, Deadly Night.

DON'T TALK TO STRANGE MEN (1962)

Don't Talk To Strange Men was directed by Pat Jackson and written by Gwen Cherrell. In a rural part of England, a female hitchhiker is found dead by some children. She has been murdered and there are reports in the newspapers of a prowler being on the loose. A schoolgirl named Jean Painter (Christina Gregg) lives in the area with her parents and younger sister Ann (Janina Faye). Jean often has to wait for a bus in a country lane after her babysitting duties at the pub her uncle owns. There is a public telephone box right next to the bus stop. When the phone rings, Jean decides to pick it up and finds herself engaged in small talk with a seemingly charming and suave man on the other end of the line.

Jean agrees to speak to the man again the next day and so this becomes a regular thing. She tells him her name is Samantha and is soon obsessed with this mystery man and can't stop talking about him to her sister. Jean has fallen in love with the voice on the phone and is eager to meet the man it belongs to. As the title of this film warns us though, Jean is naïve and foolhardy in the extreme and making a big mistake by placing so much trust in a complete stranger she knows nothing about...

Don't Talk To Strange Men only runs to just over an hour and is a bit like a feature length public information film - only in the form of a drama rather than a cartoon or some kid flying a kite near pylons. This film is ahead of its time in a sense because the man on the phone is clearly 'grooming' Jean and worming his way into her head. The fact that he is anonymous and just a voice on the line has parallels with the creepy and grim online criminal 'groomers' of today who can hide behind fake profiles, pictures, and avatars. Jean becomes giddy with romantic dreams about the wonderful man on the phone and is oblivious to the fact he's most likely some middle-aged rapist serial killer. The scenes where Jean is on the phone with the man are well acted and although very different in tone (much tamer) sort of anticipate telephone themed horror films of the future like Black Christmas.

Christina Gregg is pretty good as the schoolgirl with only one or two quibbles. Her cut glass accent makes her feel too posh for this part and she also looks too old for the role. In real life, Gregg was a married twenty-three year-old woman when she made this film. You might think that they cast older because they didn't want a genuine actor of school age to have to play this material or be put in (fictional) danger. However, Janina Faye as Jean's younger sister Ann is placed in danger near the end. You never actually see the face of the man on the phone although he does turn up in person in the end. I think this was a wise move. We see enough of him though to realise he isn't the person Jean thought he was.

When she spies him in a pub talking on the phone we can see in Jean's reaction that she realises she's been a fool and the man was just conning her when he pretended to be some charming young person on the phone. There is a very solid supporting cast in this film but best of all is the great Dandy Nichols as Molly the bus conductor. If only Jean had listened to Molly. Molly dispenses very sensible advice which Jean sadly ignores. Cyril Raymond and Gillian Lind are also good as Jean's parents. Despites its brief running time, Don't Talk To Strange Men does have a few lulls. Some of the family stuff does feel like padding at times. One thing which helps the film is that it isn't melodramatic or exploitation and tells its story in a calm and measured sort of way.

The only time the film diverts from this approach is right at the end with fisticuffs and a chase. The last act is genuinely tense and unsettling though with a chilling moment where Jean realises that through her stupidity she might have put her sister in danger. The scariest moment in the film comes when Ann tells the man she isn't Samantha. "You are to me," he replies and then comments, with a tone of creepy delight, that she's younger than he expected. I'm not quite sure if you'd call Don't Talk To Strange Men a horror film but it's pretty close. Think of this as a social message crime drama with horror elements - like the dead body at the start. Don't Talk To Strange Men is a good little film on the whole and - sadly - the main theme and message of the film is even more relevant today than it was back in 1962.

DREAM DEMON (1988)

Dream Demon was directed by Harley Cokeliss - who also co-wrote the film. Other films Cokeliss directed include Warlords of the 21st Century and Black Moon Rising. Dream Demon is a fairly obscure film which seemed to slip past largely unnoticed in 1988. This seems somewhat unfair because, while not perfect, it is a likeable and commendable effort. The story revolves around a young woman named Diana (Jemma Redgrave) who is due to marry Oliver (Mark Greenstreet). Oliver is a war hero famed for his exploits in the Falklands. He always seems to wear some sort of naval commander uniform and is rarely at home. Diana, who comes from a wealthy family, is therefore often left at a loose end at her London house. She is suffering from horrible nightmares which are so vivid they seem real. So very real - as Terry-Thomas would say in Vault of Horror.

To make matters even worse, Diana is being pestered by two scuzzy members of the press - reporter Paul (Jimmy Nail) and photographer Peck (Timothy Spall). Paul and Peck are fishing for stories about Oliver's sex life. A young American woman named Jenny (Kathleen Wilhoite) helps Diana fight off the two intrusive reporters and the women become friends. Jenny being here is no coincidence though. She was drawn to Jenny's house because she believes she has some sort of strange connection to this place. Things get even more complicated when Jenny finds herself pulled into the nightmares of Diana...

Dream Demon has a memorable opening nightmare scene with Diana about to marry Oliver in church but getting cold feet and punching him so hard his head flies off, a geyser of blood splattering all over her pristine white wedding dress. Clive Barker once said that when you make a horror film you should put something crazy at the start and then you've got the audience's attention and can tell some story for the next twenty minutes. Dream Demon takes a page from that book. This film is sometimes called a British version of A Nightmare On Elm Street and while you can see why the two films might be compared they aren't that similar - aside from the focus on nightmares which seem real. Dream Demon doesn't have a supernatural horror villain at its heart like Elm Street and it is also more of a haunted house caper.

Dream Demon also clearly draws some influences from Hellraiser. The nightmare versions of the house Diana encounters sometimes look a lot like the fog baked vaguely industrial hellscapes where the Cenobites tend to emerge from. Dream Demon has good designs and excellent special effects. Considering this is a low-budget British horror film from 1988 it looks surprisingly good today. Dream Demon was the film debut of Jemma Redgrave. These days she is probably best known for her role as Kate Lethbridge-Stewart in the increasingly unwatchable continuation of Doctor Who. Redgrave is likeable in Dream Demon and the fact she's fairly ordinary and low-key makes her quite a novel sort of horror heroine. Redgrave also has a believable friendship in the film with Kathleen Wilhoite as Jenny. Wilhoite has been in many things (E.R, Twin Peaks, Gilmore Girls etc) and is one of those actors who basically just gives the same performance in anything but if it isn't broke why fix it?

Mark Greenstreet is a very cartoon villain as Oliver but he's not in the film much. He looks like a member of Bros (there's a musical reference for the youngsters) with his peroxide crop. A few years before he made Dream Demon, Mark Greenstreet auditioned to play James Bond in The Living Daylights. When he was doing his James Bond audition at Pinewood, Greenstreet took a break to use the toilet and bumped into Michael Biehn in his Corporal Hicks colonial space marine outfit. James Cameron was shooting Aliens next door. I presume, given that Redgrave's character is named Diana, the media trying to get stories about the love life of Oliver is a reference to Prince Charles and Diana Spencer. Oliver certainly carries himself like a royal. I bet he wears that military uniform to Tesco.

If anyone steals Dream Demon it is Timothy Spall as the slobbish photographer Peck. It's a fun gimmick to get Auf Wiedersehen, Pet stars Spall and Jimmy Nail in this film as a double act. Spall is transformed into a demonic sort of character in the film but he's disgusting in human form too as he munches on chow mein in the car or makes lewd comments to Diana. You get the impression Spall had a lot of fun making this film. One sequence where Spall (in nightmare form) is eating some disgusting looking food is so horrible you can barely watch. In the film, Diana and Jenny have visions of a young girl who once lived in the house and had an abusive father. Annabelle Lanyon, who plays the child, was twenty-eight in real life and looks it. I don't quite understand why they had an adult playing this child. Maybe I missed something. By the way, I should mention Susan Fleetwood, who is good in the film as Diana's therapist.

Dream Demon empties its bag of tricks somewhere along the

line and the strange nightmare sequences do get a bit repetitive in the end but on the whole I quite enjoyed this film. It isn't what you would call a classic but it is competent and inventive and ambitious at times for a low budget eighties horror film. It probably could have been better but by the same token it could have been a lot worse too. If you are in the mood for some astral projection spooky house capers and like the idea of Jimmy Nail and Timothy Spall turning into monsters then Dream Demon could be the film for you. There are no demons in the film by the way so I don't know why this is called Dream Demon. It's a fun title though so who cares?

EXPOSE (1976)

Exposé (aka House on Straw Hill) was written and directed by James Kenelm Clarke. This is the only British film that ended up on the 'video nasty' list following the passing of the Video Recordings Act 1984. Some versions of this film are heavily edited - which sort of defeats the purpose of watching an allegedly notorious film. What is the plot of this strange film? Paul Martin (Udo Kier) is an author who had a hugely successful debut book and is now holed up in a country house somewhere in southern England to write the follow up. He lives with his girlfriend Suzanne (Fiona Richmond) but she leaves him and he hires a typist named Linda (Linda Hayden) to help him work more quickly. Paul begins to be plagued by disturbing visions. He lusts after Linda but she spurns his attention. It turns out that both of these people are hiding a big secret...

Exposé is a very odd film I must say. It is quite amateurish and badly lit but the locations are nice and the bizarre editing is not without interest. Udo Kier (surprisingly handsome as a young man with a big mop of hair) is dubbed in the film as the pretentious author having these nightmares (which seem to predict the future). It is unintentionally funny when Linda is menaced by two randy youths (who have clearly never heard of the MeToo movement) early on because they are actually played by Karl Howman and James Bond stuntman Vic Armstrong. Both are a bit on the old side to be believable as bike riding tearaways. Peter duffs both of them up in amusing fashion but when Jacko and Vic return again in the film it is not nearly as amusing because things get much darker.

The strange thing about Exposé is that the basic plot is like that of a Sunday afternoon television thriller film but the story is decorated with lots of unpleasant stuff like rape and people being shot in the face. The violence in the film has unavoidably been tamed by the passage of time. The other thing which made this film notorious in its day was presumably the nudity. Linda Hayden has plenty of nude scenes (though a body double was apparently used for some of these) and romps with Fiona Richmond in the film too. Fiona Richmond was a glamour model who made some sex comedies. She's not exactly Samantha Morton in the thesping department. Fiona Richmond having a major supporting role in this film would be a bit like someone in the early 2000s giving Jo Guest a major role in a horror film. Fiona Richmond is only in Exposé to get her kit off. Udo Kier was famously withering when later commenting on Richmond's acting ability.

The conclusion of this film (which you may or may not guess in advance - Linda is pointedly not given a surname for much of the film) is especially ludicrous. Some parts of the film are interesting but stretches of the film are quite boring too. Exposé never makes much sense and it is pretentious too at the best of times. I suppose the main problem with this film is that if you took out the sex and violence it would probably be considered a fairly tedious and (for the most part) badly acted thriller film. The actual foundations of the film, beneath the more notorious elements, are not actually that strong. The cast are attractive though and if you like blood and violence, well, you'll get that in the end. The house used in the film was apparently one being rented by the director. The house is located in Little Baddow, Essex. It looks like a nice place to live with the wheat fields out the back.

Exposé is like an ineptly made arty psychological thriller which morphs into a violent exploitation film. I don't think this film is a lost classic and it isn't really something you'd find yourself yearning to watch again in a hurry but it isn't without interest and a certain morbid curiosity. Though the film is set in the countryside and mostly populated by attractive people it has a raw, tawdry and downbeat aura to it - which makes for quite an interesting clash. Linda Hayden is quite good in the film too though she said that this is the only film she regretted making because they inserted new scenes without her consent.

Exposé is probably worth a go (so long as you aren't watching a heavily edited version) for completist purposes but I can't honestly say I'm the biggest fan of this film.

THE FIEND (1972)

The Fiend (aka Beware My Brethren) was directed by Robert Hartford-Davis. This is a rather bonkers film which turns out to be a surprising amount of fun. The plot revolves around a fundamentalist church sect (the Brethren) led by a minister. The minister is played by Patrick Magee so The Fiend is off to a fine start already. Everything is more entertaining with a dose of Patrick Magee. A daft 1970s British horror film without Patrick Magee is like hot water without tea. Strawberries without cream. Apple pie without custard. Scones without jam. I could go on but you get the general idea.

Keen members of this religious sect are the widow Birdy Wemys (Ann Todd) and her son Kenny (Tony Beckley). Kenny is sort of like the Alan Bennett character Graham from A Chip in the Sugar in that he's shy and awkward and still lives with his mum. The two things which distinguish Kenny from Graham is that Kenny is a religious nut and a serial killer. Birdy has diabetes and a nurse named Brigitte (Madeleine Hinde) is assigned to check on her. Brigitte doesn't like the sound of this church sect that Birdy and Kenny are members of and has her journalist sister Paddy (Suzanna Leigh) go and investigate...

The Fiend has most of what you might be looking for in a daft 1970s horror film. Murder, gore, sexploitation, famous faces, nutty performances, intrigue, unintentional laughs. This is a stupid film that never makes much sense but it does cross over into that zone where it is so odd it becomes quite compelling because you can't believe what you are watching. The gospel music number at the church which kicks things off is certainly a surprise. A surprise in that the music is good and this nutty church sect are not a bunch of sinister miserabilists - well, at least not on the surface. Suzanna Leigh is not terribly convincing as a journalist but she brightens any film with her mere presence so we are happy to see her anyway. Madeleine Hinde, as the nurse, didn't do a huge amount of acting but she has another entry in this book later with Incense of the Damned.

The murders in The Fiend were, I suspect, heavily inspired by the Jack the Stripper case. Hammersmith in London was the scene of a number of grisly murders in 1964 and 1965. The killer became known as Jack the Stripper because the murder victims were all prostitutes and always had their clothes and belongings (including, believe it or not, false teeth) removed. However, despite a huge police operation, the killer was never found and the murders remain a mystery to this day. The puzzling thing about the murders is that none of the victims displayed any evidence of sexual violence. The police detective heading up the search for Jack the Stripper in the 1960s predicted that the case would be as famous as the Jack the Ripper murders. He was obviously completely wrong about that. A lot of people today seem to have barely heard of Jack the Stripper.

Kenny has a day job as a lifeguard at a swimming pool in The Fiend. Now, you might be thinking that this is a surprising occupation for Kenny to hold and you'd be right about that. You couldn't imagine Graham Whittaker from A Chip in the Sugar working as a lifeguard and Kenny is equally ill at ease in such a role. Because of his religious beliefs he is disgusted by lust, sin, and sex and so if he notices any woman at the swimming pool wearing a swimming costume too skimpy for his liking he tends to give them a ticking off. How he hasn't been sacked or got a punch in the face for his trouble is a mystery. The reliable Tony Beckley is very entertaining as the bad tempered and strange Kenny. There is a smidgeon of Norman Bates in this character I think.

Ann Todd is also enjoyable as his mother Birdy. Birdy is to blame for how Kenny has turned out - although you can't really blame her for the murders. This film is not exactly a huge fan of religion. It is implied that Birdy is a repressed lesbian and the sect has very strong views on gay people. The sect also bars Birdy from using insulin to manage her diabetes because medicine is against their beliefs. She is just supposed to pray or something. It reminds of that Curb Your Enthusiasm episode where Larry David asked a Christian Scientist what he did when his telly went on the blink. Did he simply pray for it to work again?

The Fiend has a few twists at the end although you'll probably have a fair idea of where this is heading. As far as Robert Hartford-Davis films go, The Fiend is probably not quite as entertaining as Corruption but it is a lot better than Incense of the Damned (to be honest it is hard to think of ANYTHING which isn't better than Incense of the Damned). The Fiend has a few dull stretches but the murders, nudity, and 70s atmosphere make up for the lulls. I think the songs in the film get a bit annoying at times and the plot is wafer thin when held up to the light but The Fiend is definitely an experience. This is hardly a classic film and most likely not even a good one but it is very watchable and as daft as a brush to boot.

FRIGHT (1971)

Fright was directed by Peter Collinson and written by (the wonderfully named) Tudor Gates. A staple of the horror genre is the babysitter in peril film - where a young attractive female babysitter is menaced in a spooky house by some maniac. Well, many believe Fright to be the grandfather of this genre. All those films that followed, from Halloween to When a Stranger Calls, have elements which were already done by Fright. In the film, Susan George plays a student named Amanda who is babysitting for a couple named

Helen (Honor Blackman) and Jim (George Cole). Helen has an infant son named Tara - which is an odd name for a boy but that was actually the child's name in real life and he was the son of the director. Helen and Jim are off to a village eight miles away to have a meal. This leaves Amanda in their rural farmhouse alone with the child. We learn that Helen's former husband Brian (Ian Bannen) is now in a psychiatric institution because he tried to kill her. Well, you can see where this is going can't you?

Fright is very much a game of two halves for me. The opening of the film is terrific with Susan George as Amanda walking to the farmhouse alone in the fog and then being left there to look after the child. She nibbles on a biscuit, sips sherry, and is (in a great scene) spooked by a noise which turns out to a washing line snagging on a branch. Amanda's purple dress is an iconic horror heroine costume and a taut mysterious chiller surely awaits. But then, for me at least, Fright slowly begins to lose its way. The arrival of Dennis Waterman as Amanda's randy boyfriend Chris is generally fine. Babysitter in peril films which followed often use this device of having the randy boyfriend turn up but irritate the heroine and leave. Chris, as with babysitter boyfriends in numerous films, tries to spook Amanda a bit for a joke but she doesn't find it very funny.

As everyone points out, Fright has George Cole and Dennis Waterman side by side in the titles - several years before they made a legendary television double act in Minder. Sadly though, George and Dennis don't have any scenes together in Fright. Chris gives Amanda some backstory on Helen's former husband Brian. Chris, very tactfully, tells Amanda he heard in the village that Brian is in the "nut house" because he's a "nutter". Anyway, Fright starts really well and establishes this premise of Susan George as a babysitter alone in a farmhouse on a dark night. That's all you need really. There's your film right there. Susan George is charismatic enough to carry this film, her reactions are expressive, the house is spooky, the garden is creepy. Just introduce the maniac trying to get in, make the phone line go dead, and you've got a cult classic in the making.

It is at this point though that Fright begins to make a number of frustrating and somewhat baffling decisions. There is way too much time, for example, given to Helen and Jim having dinner in some pub (which the film tries to depict as posh but isn't really). Helen endlessly worries about leaving her son with a babysitter when her ex-husband is a maniac in the nut house, sorry, I mean a psychiatric institution. Helen worries that Brian might escape. John Gregson as Dr Cordell has come out to dinner with them and assures Helen that Brian is safely locked up. She has to move on with her life. You get the impression that the length of these scenes had something to do with giving Honor Blackman more screen time. I must say though I did enjoy the scene where all the old people in the pub are dancing to disco music.

The introduction of Brian into the film proper marks the moment where Fright turns from taut babysitter chiller into something of a mess. Brian is just a face at the window and presence in the garden at first and this worked great. As soon as Brian enters the house and Ian Bannen starts maniacally chewing the scenery up, Fright soon begins to outstay its welcome. Susan George is no longer the central focus of the film. She's now reduced to standing there reacting as Ian Bannen (in a terrible wig) hams it up to oblivion.

Fright also begins to grate with strange script decisions. Like when Amanda calls the pub to report an emergency and the phone goes dead. Helen could tell it was an upset young girl on the phone but she's persuaded by Jim and Dr Cordell to forget about it and enjoy her evening. What? The end of the film is also preposterous.

I loved the first sections of this film but then found the last half a slog as it lurches into melodrama (the frazzled Brian muddles Amanda up with Helen so he keeps seeing Honor Blackman's face when he's with Susan George), a few too many scenes with the police, and then a hostage drama at the end. I don't know if I'm alone in thinking that Fright would have been perfectly fine just keeping its focus on Susan George as the babysitter and made the threat to her her more mysterious rather than have Ian Bannen waltz in and give us a stock crazy person. By the way, there is not a drop of Arthur Daley in George Cole's performance here - which shows how good he was. Maurice Kaufmann, who plays the police chief, was married to Honor Blackman when Fright was made. Look out for Trigger from Fools and Horses (Roger Lloyd-Pack) as one of the police constables.

This film probably would have been one of the last things John Gregson did. He doesn't have a lot to do in the film to apart from drink gin and tonic and eat prawn cocktails with George Cole's Jim. I love the way Jim has sherry at home before leaving for the pub and then orders a scotch when he arrives. He is then seen drinking wine and more besides. Later on he gets in his car to drive home. Did they not have laws about drinking and driving in 1974? Fright is a mixed bag for me. Parts of the film are great but it does lose its way in the end. There is a bit of blood in the film but not much. The most disturbing part of the film is when the child is threatened with a shard of glass. By the way, the film Amanda is watching on television in the house is Hammer's Plague of the Zombies.

THE FROZEN DEAD (1966)

When it comes to cryogenics, I am reminded of the sage words of Rigsby in Rising Damp. Rigsby was against cryogenics. He said no one was putting him in there with the fish fingers. Rigbsy would definitely have been against the research undertaken by Dr Norberg (Dana Andrews) in The Frozen Dead - which was written and directed by Herbert J. Leder.

Dr Norberg is a Nazi scientist who for twenty years since the war has been experimenting on how to revive Nazi soldiers he put into deep freeze when the war ended. Norberg lives in London and poses as a respectable doctor (the fact he was an administrator at a concentration camp is something he keeps quiet about) who does pioneering work in organ preservation.

However, there is a secret group of Nazis who are desperate to revive the Third Reich and Dr Norberg is their biggest hope. Norberg has successfully worked out how to revive a frozen dead person but restoring the brain to a functional working state is a much peskier problem and one he hasn't manage to solve yet. Norberg's assistant Karl (Alan Tilvern) comes up with an extreme solution in order to speed things up...

You could say that The Frozen Dead was somewhat ahead of its time given that Nazi themed zombie and horror films are ten a penny these days - at least in the world of low-budget streaming films. The Frozen Dead is a truly preposterous film but it is played fairly straight by the cast and directed in staid plodding fashion. This is one of those films that turns out to be nowhere near as entertaining as its synopsis makes it sound. This is a very cheap film and plays out almost entirely in a few rooms and Dr Norberg's lab. There is one scene though at a train station where you see a nice old train. At nearly 100 minutes this film feels way too long to me.

Norberg's niece Jean (Anna Palk) is staying at the house with her friend Elsa (Kathleen Breck) and Karl murders Elsa so that Dr Norberg will have a brain to experiment on. Jean turns detective to try and find out what happened to Elsa and the scenes of her investigating do tend to act as a drag on the film because, with respect to Anna Palk, we are here for the frozen Nazi brain experiment capers and not Miss Marple. Elsa ends up as a blue head on a table with a plastic bowl over her brain and electrodes. She can't speak so just has to faintly moan. You can't thinking that Kathleen Breck's retirement from acting the following year had something to do with this film. There must be easier ways to make a living than playing a mute blue head.

On the wall of the lab are arms and legs that Norberg has kept alive as part of his experiments. You just KNOW there will be a payoff for these arms and legs and so it transpires. Dana Andrews, who was a pretty big star in his youth, struggles to conceal his boredom in this film. There is a very tightly contested contest between Andrews and the rest of the cast over who can do the worst German accent. I must say that the plans of the Nazis in this film do not stand up to close scrutiny. Even if they revive 1,500 Nazis, as planned, how is that going to enable them to take over the world in 1966? It doesn't make any sense.

Philip Gilbert as Dr Ted Roberts looks a bit like a wonky clone of Sean Connery and is supposed to be one of the few nice people in the film. it's not easy to warm to him though because he experiments on animals as part of his own research. He is invited to meet Dr Norberg, takes a shine to Jean, and then gets mixed up in this frozen Nazi palaver going on in the basement. By the way, look out for Edward Fox as one the revived Nazis that Norbert keeps locked in a room like mental patients. Fox doesn't have any lines because the revived Nazis can't talk on account of Norberg not yet having any idea how to repair their brains.

The revived Nazis do have fragments on their memories though and hone in one specific memory, however trivial, in their mind and do this over and over again. One man is constantly bouncing an imaginary ball for example. I like to think the cast of The Frozen dead all burst into laughter each time the director yelled "Cut!" - overwhelmed by the ludicrous premise of this film. Despite my affectionate ribbing of this film I did find it reasonably watchable for a good chunk of the running time although it does go on too long to completely sustain one's interest for the whole duration.

The frozen Nazis in the freezer makes for an arresting image and Alan Tilvern brings some welcome ham to the part of Karl. Kathleen Breck does as well as can be expected in the role of a mute telepathic blue head. You can't help thinking though that a horror film about Nazis trying to revive frozen people and take over the world should really be a lot more fun than The Frozen Dead.

There is something slightly odd about The Frozen Dead in that this is a daft film but it doesn't feel like the cast and director are in on the joke. The cast playing a daft horror film in straight fashion can work wonderfully well (look at the original 1950s version of The Fly) but for some reason it doesn't really work here.

FULL CIRCLE (1977)

Full Circle (aka The Haunting of Julia) was directed by Richard Loncraine and written by Harry Bromley Davenport (yes, Mr Xtro himself). The film is based on the novel Julia by Peter Straub - which I must confess I've never read. Full Circle got quite mixed reviews and became a rather forgotten film. I find this rather odd because this is one of the best British horror films of the 1970s. The story concerns a woman named Julia (Mia Farrow). Julia suffers a tragedy when her young daughter Katie (Sophie Ward) starts choking in the kitchen. Julia panics and tries to perform a tracheotomy (which is mercifully left offscreen) but Katie dies as a consequence. We cut to months later. The devastated and guilt ridden Julia is now separated from her husband Magnus (Keir Dullea) and has moved into an old house. She begins to detect the ghostly presence of a girl in the house. After a seance, Julia also because obsessed with solving the mystery of a little boy who a psychic medium claimed to see...

It's probably best to go into this film knowing nothing. Full Circle is often compared to Don't Look Now and you can understand why because they are both framed around grief and guilt and lives that were shattered by the death of a child. Mia Farrow was apparently quite reluctant to do this film because due to being so well known for Rosemary's Baby she didn't want to become known as a horror actress. She did obviously relent in the end and the fragile and almost ephemeral quality she had in her younger years works perfectly in this film. Not long after Full Circle, Farrow began a relationship with Woody Allen and appeared in films for him until the early 1990s. Although the personal side of their relationship did not end well (to put it mildly), Farrow showed what a great and surprisingly versatile actor she could be in films like Broadway Danny Rose and The Purple Rose of Cairo.

It's a shame Full Circle isn't well known because Farrow gives one of her best performances - the sadness of Julia seeping out of the film at every turn and becoming almost unbearable. You could probably describe this as an arthouse horror film and at times not even a horror film at all. I absolutely adore the moody piano/electronic music score in this film by Colin Towns. Shots of rain on a car window and Mia Farrow staring off into space become hypnotic and strangely entrancing. I fell under the spell of Full Circle but I can see how this film might not be for everyone. Some people seem to find this film slow and a bit plodding. Julia becomes obsessed in the film with the mystery of a girl named Olivia - who seems to be inspired by the notorious Mary Bell (the eleven year-old girl who murdered two small boys in Newcastle in 1968). It might just be a coincidence but Peter Straub, though American, did spend time living in London so it is possible he might have heard of Mary Bell.

Julia's investigations become very absorbing in the film because you aren't quite sure where this is all going. I gather changes were made from the novel - the fates of a few characters being changed. Tom Conti lends able support in the film as antiques shop owner Mark Berkeley. Mark is Julia's best friend. You fear some sappy romantic subplot between the pair but the film sensibly avoids this and just has them as friends. Edward Hardwicke (Dr Watson in the Jeremy Brett series of Sherlock Holmes television adventures) has a memorable cameo - as too does Peter Sallis. Lou Beale from EastEnders (Anna Wing) is the psychic and Jill Bennett and Robin Gammell are also good in the film. The only duff scene for me is when Julia visits the psychic Mrs Flood and the niece sounds like Dick Van Dyke in Mary Poppins.

It is interesting how old films date in different ways. There is a scene in Full Circle for example where Julia goes to a playground and sits taking polaroid's of the children playing. If someone sat themselves in a public place and started taking photographs of children today they'd end up being spoken to by the police I'd imagine. The thing I love as much as anything about old films is that no one has a mobile telephone or the internet. Julia has to go to a lovely old library to read newspapers for her research.

The title of the film becomes very apt when we reach the end. One of the interesting things about the film is that it retains an ambiguous quality. Mia Farrow said she didn't approach this as a horror film at all and played it as a drama about the mental disintegration of a person who has has suffered the worst tragedy that can befall anyone - the loss of a child. It is really up to the viewer how they wish to read this film and up to them too what they take from it. Anyone expecting more of an overt horror film might be disappointed because Full Circle is not The Omen - despite a few Omen style deaths. If you do fall for the sad, poignant, and strange spell cast by the film though you should find this an unforgettable experience. Full Circle is like a strange, lost little masterpiece of seventies horror cinema and deserves to be more famous than it ever became.

FUNNY MAN (1994)

Funny Man was written and directed by Simon Sprackling. A smug music producer named Max Taylor (Benny Young) wins the mansion belonging to Callum Chance (Christopher Lee) in a game of poker. Max is pretty happy about this but in reality it turns out to be the worst thing that could ever happen. He travels to the mansion with his wife Tina (Ingrid Lacey) and son and daughter to take a look. However, it transpires that the house contains some sort of demon who lives in a strange cartoon world underneath the house. The demon is known as Funny Man (played by Tim James) and is a grotesque and diminutive jester who resembles Mr Punch. The stock in trade of Funny Man is killing people in darkly comical ways. Max and his family are not the only people in danger because an eclectic gaggle of hitchhikers end up in the house too thanks to

Max's brother Jamie (Jamie Heard) driving them there. Suffice to say, the body count soon piles up as Funny Man begins his work...

I gather that Funny Man was conceived as a very straight horror film but then became a comedic horror film to lean more into the strengths of Tim James as the title character. James (who doesn't seem to have done too much acting besides this film) is very good as the title character - who is sort of like a cross between Freddy Krueger and Les Dawson. This is a very British end of the pier supernatural horror villain as far as supernatural horror villains go. Funny Man constantly breaks the fourth wall to chat to us and offer a running commentary on his grisly deeds and while a lot of the humour is low-brow and childish there are some amusing moments and a few scenes so strange they become oddly compelling. Funny Man even murders Max's children but all the same you sort of root for Funny Man. What probably helps us root for Funny Man is that most of the other characters are so annoying. You don't really lament the loss of any of these people - which was maybe the point.

This film seems to be pretty much loathed (a dismal 4.4 on IMDB) but it does have its moments. Funny Man listening to Steve Wright on the radio at the end as he takes a moment to reflect on his work ("still... turned out nice again..."), electrocuting the daughter as she plays on a Game Boy, a bizarre scene where one of the characters is killed by a comedy prop bomb at a seaside Punch & Judy show, and - perhaps the most famous sequence - Funny Man blowing (quite literally) a character's brain out with a duck hunting gun. While there is plenty of gore the impact of the murders is lessened by the broad comic tone of the film. It is an odd clash of tones because there is some nasty stuff in the film but we aren't being asked to take any of this seriously. Benny Young as Max Taylor is one of the few people in the film required to give anything resembling a performance. Most of the cast seem to be trying to mesh with the tongue-in-cheek nature of the film and offer little more than surreal 'turns' rather than acting performances.

The worst performance in the film comes from Rhona Cameron - who is dressed like Thelma from Scooby-Doo and even named Thelma in the film. Cameron simply pulls a number of funny faces. The singer Pauline Black is a 'Psychic commando' who becomes the main threat to Funny Man in the house. Black gives a very cartoon performance but her showdown with Funny Man in his twisted smurf like world beneath the mansion is sort of fun. Chris Walker (billed as the Hard Man) is one of the few cast members here you'll recognise as he's been in stuff like The Bill and Coronation Street. Walker's character has one of the weirdest vignettes in the film when he is lured into a strip club that Funny Man has knocked up in the mansion grounds - with Funny Man as the stripper. Walker's character doesn't seem too phased by the club being populated only by a gargoyle looking court jester but then Funny Man is that sort of film.

I think one of the problems with Funny Man is that it sometimes feels like a big private joke that the director and cast are in on but the audience are not. You'd imagine they had a lot of fun making this film and just threw in lots of crazy stuff that made them laugh or felt like a good idea at the time after one too many light ales. I do though like the conspiratorial style of Funny Man where, like an old fashioned northern comic, he takes us into his confidence and mutters asides and jokes. Sometimes, when he can't think of anything to say, Funny Man will just look at the camera and shrug his shoulders. There must be an alternative universe where this became a franchise and Funny Man went into space for the fourth one. Some parts of this film are amateurish and bewildering while other parts are quite effective. Funny Man's first introduction is pretty good. He ambles up behind Mrs Taylor, makes awkward small talk, and even takes in some art while she runs away - secure in the knowledge that she is trapped and will always end up back in that room.

There's a sort of twist near the end of Max having ripped off his brother Jamie in the music world, which makes Max being tormented by Funny Man karma and just desserts - though this hardly condones Funny Man killing Max's kids! Anyway, this plot thread leads to a frankly perplexing and bizarre climax where Funny Man allows to Jamie to live out his lost pop star dreams for a moment. Funny Man turns DJ and is made to resemble Jimmy Savile - a joke that obviously doesn't play very well these days. Funny Man is strange, inconsistent, amateurish, fun in places, badly acted by much of the cast, but, for better or for worse, a fairly unique sort of experience. To be honest with you, I don't think I'm ever going to get that Funny Man song with the school choir out of my head. Funny Man seems to be a very Marmite sort of horror film. Most people hate it but it does have a small following too. It is probably worth a look though if only for the strange and amusing performance by Tim James as Funny Man. By the way, I wouldn't get too excited about Christopher Lee having prominent billing because he's only in it for two scenes. Gerry Anderson fans will note the presence of Ed Bishop as one of the poker players at the start of the film.

HAUNTED (1995)

Haunted is a film adaptation of the novel of the same name by the late James Herbert. The film had a number of writers and was directed by the veteran Lewis Gilbert. Gilbert directed many films in his career - including Alfie, Educating Rita, and three Bond films. Haunted was the penultimate film of Gilbert's long career. Though a handsome production with a good cast, Haunted seems to be fairly forgotten these days. It's an old fashioned ghost story and certainly watchable if nothing amazing. The film takes place in 1928 and concerns a professor named David Ash (Aidan Quinn) who works in parapsychology. Ash is basically a debunker of the paranormal. He's a bit like the James Randi of his day you could say.

Ash is haunted by the death of his twin sister Juliet (played by Victoria Shalet) - who died while still a child. He is implored to come to a country house named Edbrook. The request is from Tess Webb (Anna Massey). Webb claims she is being tormented by ghosts. It turns out that Tess Webb is a nanny at the house to the Mariell siblings - Christina (Kate Beckinsale), Robert (Anthony Andrews), and Simon (Alex Lowe). As he settles into the house to investigate, Ash becomes taken with Christina Mariell and you can't really blame him given that she looks like a young Kate Beckinsale. What is the explanation for the secrets this house seems to have up its sleeve?

I recall reading the book version of Haunted by James Herbert while growing up and can remember reading quite a few James Herbert novels. He never got the acclaim or critical credibility of someone like Clive Barker but Herbert's books were undemanding gore drenched fun. I've no idea how these books would hold up up if I read them today but I happily devoured things like The Fog and his Rats trilogy as a youngster. Herbert apparently came up with Haunted as an idea for a BBC script but then turned it into a novel. There are a lot of differences between the book and film and if you do love the book you might find some of these changes irritating.

For one thing, James Herbert's novel is set in the present day (1988) whereas this film is set in 1928. I can only presume the makers of the film felt there would be nothing too interesting about setting the film in the present day and wanted more of a period ghost atmosphere. However, there is very nothing novel about setting ghost stories in the past either. From a modern vantage point today a ghost story set in 1995 or 1988 might have been more fun to watch than one set in 1928. The other big difference here is the main character. In the novel David Ash (who I believe Herbert used in a trilogy - I only ever read the first book) is a seedy sort of character who has a drinking problem. You could imagine someone like Timothy Spall in this part (or I could anyway). In the film though he's played by the handsome Aidan Quinn. I suspect this was one of those productions where they were ordered to get an American lead actor in for funding and commercial reasons. Quinn is ok in the film but he's a bit bland. He doesn't really do much with the role.

The film also adds an incest subplot which I definitely don't remember from the book. By the way, the casting here is funny today because one of the siblings (Simon) is played by Alex Lowe. Lowe is best known these days for playing Clinton Baptiste. Clinton Baptiste is a psychic medium and a comedy spoof on that strange world of grifters and frauds who pretend they can talk to the dead. I always used to admire the chutzpah of the late Derek Acorah when he pretended to get possessed by a spirit on Most Haunted. He was such a terrible actor and always did the same voice! Anyway, why are we talking about Derek Acorah? Let's get back to Haunted.

Haunted is a competent and nice looking film that is generally fine for what it is. You could imagine sitting through this on the telly and not being too bored. The problem is though that it never becomes much more than this. What didn't help I suppose is that, having read the book, I was aware of what the main twist in the story was going to be. I suspect you'll probably work it out for yourself anyway even if you haven't read the book. It isn't exactly the most original or unexpected of twists. There are some great actors in supporting roles here. John Gielgud, Anna Massey, Liz Smith, Geraldine Somerville. Kate Beckinsale is given a lot of screen time as Christina. You can see that the makers of this film think Beckinsale is their trump card and destined for stardom. Anthony Andrews smirks away in the background as Robert Mariell.

Haunted is certainly a watchable film but ultimately it's a trifle rote and by the numbers to ever become anything that might stick in the memory. This is one of those films that you completely forget about once the end credits roll. The film isn't particularly scary but it is quite nicely made. I think a problem with this film is that the 1928 (and country mansion) setting makes it feel like very generic oldy period ghost story caper. In the novel Ash has a car and ducks into 1980s pubs. On the whole, I personally would rather have had this film set in 1988 (or even 1995) than 1928. Haunted might even be fun today if set in the 1980s. The 1928 setting just makes it feel like your bog standard period ghost mystery.

THE HOUND OF THE BASKERVILLES (2002)

Yet another version of The Hound of the Baskervilles, this one directed by David Attwood and originally transmitted on the BBC in 2002 with much fanfare about being a fresh gritty new take on the story. It seems to have been somewhat forgotten these days though. Once again Sherlock Holmes and Dr John Watson - here in the form of Richard Roxburgh and Ian Hart - must pit their wits against the ancient legend of the Baskerville curse that is said to roam the wild moors of Dartmoor. When what is suggested to be a gigantic and terrifying hell-hound claims the life of its latest Baskerville in remote Devon, local physician Dr Mortimer (John Nettles) visits Holmes and Watson at 221b Baker Street and implores them to investigate this spooky mystery. A somewhat unconvinced looking Holmes explains that he has pressing business in London but decides - for the time being - to send Dr Watson alone to Dartmoor with his trusty revolver to keep watch over young Sir Henry Baskerville (Matt Day), the heir to the Baskerville estate.

An ambitious version of the endlessly filmed story, this version looks great at times but doesn't quite hit the mark with its habit of playing fast and loose with the story and one or two casting quibbles. What is undeniable is that the Moors described by Conan Doyle have never looked so bleak and wonderfully rugged and wild onscreen as they do here with some excellent location work in Cumbria and on the Isle of Man. The adaptation opens in compellingly atmospheric fashion with Dr Mortimer seen performing the autopsy and attending the inquest into the death of the latest Baskerville - Sir Charles - who was literally frozen in fear when found. The camera pans away from the small inquest hearing over to a rain splattered window where we look out at a desolate sweep of blustery moorland and a siren sounds, the credits rolling as an escaped prisoner is pursued across the treacherous mire.

The attempts to do something slightly new with the story don't always work but there are some nice moments and flourishes in the film. Baker Street (shot on location at Canning Street in Liverpool) looks perfect too with all the authentic Victorian hustle and bustle of horse drawn carriages and period costumes. When we meet Holmes and Watson for the first time though it soon becomes somewhat apparent that the casting of Richard Roxburgh as Holmes might not have been the most brilliant move in the world, at least for traditionalists. Roxburgh, who I believe is Australian, never quite seems fully in control of his posh English period accent and also appears rather diminutive to be Sherlock Holmes - who he looks absolutely nothing like with his short fair hair. Actors like Jeremy Brett and Basil Rathbone looked like Sherlock Holmes and Roxburgh doesn't and it's as simple as that.

Although Roxburgh gives a decentish performance and is certainly a commanding presence at times, this element of cognitive dissonance did bug me. When Holmes meets Richard E Grant's eccentric local amateur archaeologist Stapleton, Grant towers over the shortish Roxburgh and seems to have far more in the way of Holmesian looks, energy and curiosity. You unavoidably find yourself wondering why they didn't just cast Grant as Holmes instead. Was that too obvious? Roxburgh plays Holmes as a very sure of himself man of action but lacks a bit of the quirky eccentricity that the best interpretations of the character down the years have included. He dispenses a manic laugh once or twice but that's about it. They also tend to over egg the cocaine aspect to Holmes in this film I feel. In the books Holmes springs to life when he has a fresh case but sometimes resorts to cocaine during stretches of intense boredom. In this version, Roxburgh's Holmes seems to use cocaine for inspiration when he has to think about something and shoots up so frequently it feels more like Trainspotting than Sherlock Holmes on occasion.

Ian Hart is a solid, dependable Watson and very good in the film on the whole but he does lack a bit of warmth and doesn't have an awful amount of chemistry with Roxburgh's Holmes. You do slightly struggle to accept that these two men are trusted old friends who share the same flat - especially when Watson tells Holmes he doesn't trust him and also mocks Holmes' lack of knowledge in any subject that doesn't pertain to one of his cases at a dinner party. Holmes is of course offscreen for much of The Hound of the Baskervilles as Watson investigates alone for a time. As ever the Victorian trappings are great fun with cosy roaring fires, old-fashioned bedrooms and everyone eating an elaborate breakfast each morning. Matt Day is a little wooden perhaps as Henry Baskerville but Richard E Grant livens things up whenever he appears as Stapleton and Neve McIntosh lends solid support as the mysterious Miss Stapleton.

The subplot involving strange goings on on the moor which may or not involve butler and housekeeper Mr and Mrs Barrymore - competently played by Ron Cook and Liza Tarbuck - is still here but altered somewhat with some additional and possibly unnecessary dialogue at a particularly key moment. The ending too is changed in one or two ways which, while mildly interesting, aren't completely satisfying. Sherlock Holmes loses a little of his sheen in this adaption and comes across as a slightly less mythic character. One big change is the depiction of the Hound - which was essentially a big dog with fake fur in all the other adaptions. This adaption seems to suggest it really is some kind of unexplained, gigantic hell-hound creature that blusters out of the fog to kill people on command! CGI is deployed for the Hound and the results are so-so.

Much better is a moment during a seance where the Hound - or at least an animatronic paw - suddenly appears at a window out of the dark for a second. There are some excellent moments in the film but it never quite all falls together into a completely satisfying whole. Overall, this is frustrating near miss that is still laudably ambitious and certainly one of the best looking adaptions of this enduringly famous tale.

A HOUSE IN NIGHTMARE PARK (1973)

The House in Nightmare Park was directed by Peter Sykes and written by Terry Nation and Clive Exton. Comedy horror films set in mansions are not easy to do. A great many of them (like, for example, Saturday the 14th and Haunted Honeymoon) are absolutely tedious but The House in Nightmare Park is surprisingly good in that it is both funny and atmospheric. In the film, the great Frankie Howerd plays a vain ham actor named Foster Twelvetrees who is invited to a spooky country mansion by the mysterious Henderson family to perform a dramatic reading. Once he arrives at the house, Twelvetrees finds everyone to be alarmingly odd and secrets abounding. A mystery ensues and it all might have something to do with diamonds...

This film didn't do very well and isn't very famous although I have seen it on television a couple of times so it isn't what you would describe as obscure. Although he is better known for Up Pompeii and a couple of Carry Ons, in many ways The House in Nightmare Park is the quintessential Frankie Howerd performance. In his other films from this era, Frankie is usually mocking the production he is in and constantly breaking the fourth wall to talk to the camera. While this was always fun, placing him here in a more conventional film where he can't do that works wonderfully well at times. Frankie Howerd, while still unmistakably Frankie Howerd in this film, is slightly more restrained than normal and so fits into a Gothic horror spoof surprisingly well.

I suspect that Frankie was a fan of Bob Hope because he adopts a similar persona to the one Hope used in his old films - that of a joke dispensing coward who is thrust into an unusual situation. The clash between the Frankie Howerd 'persona' and the stuffy humourless Henderson family is always amusing. This film starts in fine style with Twelvetrees performing a reading on the stage. Although he is giving it his all, the crowd consists of about five people - some of whom are small boys making farting noises. Twelvetrees theatrically comes back to take another bow and finds nearly everyone has gone. The comic deflation of the pomposity of Twelvetrees is good stuff.

Frankie has some nice lines in the film (I like the moment where he says he had a packet of crisps on the train and will take a drink to wash the bits from his teeth) and his verbal jousting with Hugh Burden as Reggie Henderson is a particular highlight. A classic scene in the film has a duel between Twelvetrees and Reggie Henderson over the food at the breakfast buffet - Twelvetrees ending up with simply an egg and a piece of rock hard toast. Ray Milland is the biggest guest star in the film as Stewart Henderson and because Milland plays his role completely straight it makes for an amusing contrast when he's in a scene with Frankie. There is an epic battle of toupees going on too.

What helps this film a lot is that the direction and sets are very good and manage to create an authentic spooky house atmosphere. The film isn't scary in the least but then you probably never expected it to be. It's a Frankie Howerd comedy and not The Haunting. Rosalie Crutchley, who the British horror and sex comedy industry kept busy in the early seventies, is fine as Jessica Henderson and gives Frankie a female character to play against. Frankie Howerd's comic persona is funny in that he's a fey and camp sort of comedian and was gay in real life (though not openly gay - it was a lot more difficult for famous people to be gay in those days and, sadly, was seen as being detrimental to one's career) and he sort of sends this up on screen by portraying a sex obsessed ladies man. There's less of the sex obsessed ladies man in this film but there are still flickers of it.

One element in the film that is dated today is the white English actor John Bennett being blacked up to play the Indian manservant Patel. You obviously couldn't do that today. The House in Nightmare Park has a surprisingly weird and unsettling scene where the Henderson family are face-painted to perform a marionette lullaby musical as dolls. This scene is like something out of The League of Gentlemen television show. Ray Milland seems to be made up as a golliwog during this dance - which is another thing that dates this film. I believe that Oakley Court (a Victorian Gothic country house in the civil parish of Bray) was used for this film. A lot of horror films have used Oakley Court.

The House in Nightmare Park is probably longer than it needed to be and does get a trifle samey in the end but on the whole this is decent undemanding fun. It works better than a great many horror spoofs I've endured and gives Frankie Howerd what was probably his best ever film role.

HOUSE OF MORTAL SIN (1976)

House of Mortal Sin (aka The Confessional) was directed by Pete Walker and scripted by David McGillivray. Though reasonably well known in British horror buff circles, House of Mortal Sin seems to be less well known than House of Whipcord and Frightmare and never built up much of a reputation or following. This is slightly odd really because House of Mortal Sin is pretty good stuff and a very solid addition to Walker's CV. The story revolves around Jenny Welch (Susan Penhaligon). Jenny's sister Vanessa (Stephanie Beacham) begins to have a tentative romance with a Catholic priest name Bernard (Norman Eshley). Bernard is an old friend of Jenny but when she looks for him in church she unwittingly ends up talking to Father Meldrum (Anthony Sharp) in confession and, well, confessing a few things.

To cut a long story short, it turns out that Father Meldrum is as mad as a hatter. He becomes obsessed with Jenny and is an advocate of divine justice. The people in Jenny's life (and Jenny too) are now in grave danger from this murderous man of the cloth. The big problem for Jenny is that Father Meldrum is a respected pillar of the community and a crafty old swine to boot. Will she be able to convince anyone he is dangerous?

Father Xavier Meldrum is one of the great unsung horror villains. This is a man who will kill anyone who stands in his way and he's a smart villain too who knows how to cover his tracks. In this horror film the psychopath villain hides in plain sight. What could make a serial killer less inconspicuous than being an elderly priest? Anthony Sharp gives a remarkable performance as the disturbed Meldrum and has some great moments in the film - especially towards the end. The explanation for why he is obsessed with Jenny is quite clever and even strangely poignant when it is revealed. Meldrum's murders are (intentionally would one would presume) quite amusing as they are religious themed. An old lady who got suspicious about Father Meldrum after her daughter died is poisoned by communion wafers and the incense burner murder is a particular highlight.

Father Meldrum shares his house with housekeeper Miss Brabazon (Sheila Keith) and his elderly mute mother (Hilda Barry). Meldrum's mother is basically a hostage and plainly well aware that her son is a fruitcake. Even worse for Mrs Meldrum is that Miss Brabazon loathes her (for reasons later explained). Sheila Keith, with eyepatch glasses which make her look like a baddie from Nazi Germany, is deliciously dry and deadpan as the sarcastic Miss Brabazon. There is an excellent cast generally in this film. Norman Eshley, best known as the snooty neighbour in George & Mildred, is surprisingly good as Father Bernard Cutler. Bernard begins to fall in love with Vanessa so has to decide whether or not to leave his position at the church. He begins to investigate Meldrum on Jenny's behest and the scenes he has with Anthony Sharp are very well acted.
Stephanie Beacham (no stranger to horror) is excellent as Vanessa and I like too Stewart Bevan as Jenny's boyfriend Terry. Bevan was in all manner of things but I always remember him the most for a couple of episodes of Public Eye he was in with Alfred Burke. Susan Penhaligon is the heart of the film as Jenny and she's up to the task, proving to be a likeable and very human heroine. Penhaligon was a bit of a sex symbol (what amazing eyes) in the 1970s but never became a star or a big name. She did have a fun and eclectic run of cult work though - Patrick, Soldier of Orange, Doctor Who, The Uncanny, Tales of the Unexpected, Count Dracula, The Land That Time Forgot.

The one part of the film which does threaten to become frustrating is when Meldrum is wandering around murdering everyone like Jack the Ripper but Jenny can't get anyone to believe this priest is a lunatic (this part of the film does seem to be riffing on Rosemary's Baby). House of Mortal Sin's central story concept of someone in a position of moral authority or influence secretly abusing this position and turning out to be an awful person in real life is sadly even more topical today than it was in 1976. We've seen a fair few real priests turn out to be wrong 'uns. Not just priests either.

House of Mortal Sin has some themes on the constrictive nature of the Catholic church, which Meldrum, with his elastic and self-serving interpretation of morality and duty, tries to both blame for his actions and use to his advantage but I don't think this film is to be taken too seriously. Pete Walker always said that people read too much into his films and they are just supposed to be entertaining rather than festooned with messages (though whether he was being entirely serious about his films not having messages is open to question).

The role of Father Meldrum was apparently written with Peter Cushing in mind but he was too busy in the end. Peter Cushing would have been terrific as Meldrum but it didn't turn out too bad because you can't imagine anyone could have played this part as well as Anthony Sharp does. House of Mortal Sin is probably a trifle too long for its own good but on the whole this is very watchable with some memorable murders, a great cast, and a typically twisted Pete Walker last act. Frightmare is Walker's best horror film and House of Mortal Sin never really threatens to knock that off its perch but, taken on its own terms, House of Mortal Sin is not bad at all.

HOUSE OF MYSTERY (1961)

House of Mystery was directed by Vernon Sewell. It is based on L'Angoisse, a French play by Pierre Mills and Celia de Vilyars which Sewell had the rights to and adapted a number of times. Vernon Sewell doesn't have a tremendously stellar reputation when it comes to horror but House of Mystery is certainly not bad. This was shown in the United States as an episode of Kraft Mystery Theatre. House of Mystery is only fifty minutes long so in terms of length is more like an episode of an anthology show than a feature film. The fact that this film is so short works to its advantage. If it had been eighty minutes long I think it might have threatened to outstay its welcome in the end. You don't always need a long running time to tell a satisfying story. Just ask Rod Serling or Roald Dahl.

The premise of the film has Alan (Ronald Hines) and his wife (Colette Wilde) visiting a lovely cottage for sale in the countryside. The house seems to for sale at an unusually low price and the couple are understandably curious to know why it is going so cheap. You'd probably be a bit suspicious too if you found your dream house at a bargain price. You'd assume there had to be a catch somewhere. It turns out there IS a strange history concerning this house - which may have left it with a vengeful ghost. This would explain why they seem to having so much trouble trying to find someone to flog this house to.

An electronics expert named Mark Lemming (Peter Dyneley) - who previously owned the house - perished when he was (appropriately enough) electrocuted. Anyway, we get a flashback of how Mark haunted a couple who used to live in the house and then we get another flashback concerning what Mark did to his unfaithful wife and her lover. House of Mystery is rather an obscure film but it is quite good fun and has a clever structure with the flashbacks within flashbacks. One thing which makes this different from your bog standard haunted house story is that Mark haunts the house in electrical fashion - even appearing on the television at one point. Sure you get lights going on and off - which isn't exactly original - but the general electrical stuff is good and the electric themed fate Mark devises for his wife and her lover is like something out of a Twilight Zone episode or Hammer House of Mystery & Suspense.

House of Mystery is not especially scary (you can see why they used this as a television episode in America as it was never likely to offend anyone or terrify them) but it does hold your attention and is well made for what it is. The film has quite a lot of charm today as a period piece. After the intro with the couple viewing the house we go back to see what happened to the previous occupants of the house - a couple played by Maurice Kaufmann and Nanette Newman. Ghost investigator Mr Burdon (Colin Gordon) turns up to help and psychic Mrs Bucknall (Molly Urquhart). Mr Burdon is rather ahead of his time with his ghost hunting gadgets.

In the one of the flashbacks, we see that Mark Lemming has a black milkman. The milkman is concerned when he notices the previous day's milk hasn't been taken indoors yet and checks to see if Lemming is alright or has had an accident. Around this time, if you saw a black actor in a British horror film they were usually playing voodoo dispensing African natives or something so House of Mystery is to be commended for putting a black character in the role of a decent, ordinary person. It is actually quite charming to see a bobby on the beat (on a bicycle) in this film. Police officers seem to look so scruffy and generic today but in old British films they were always impeccably turned out and distinctive. There's a bit of murder mystery in the flashbacks and while it all leads to a fairly predictable ending the film is always very watchable and fairly enjoyable.

If this was an episode of one of those old anthology shows like The Outer Limits or Alfred Hitchcock and you watched this you'd be reasonably satisfied I think. You wouldn't think it was a classic episode but you'd probably consider it to be a decent and diverting enough one. The fact that House of Mystery is short for a film and doesn't take up a huge amount of your time makes it all the more agreeable and easy to watch. I wouldn't pretend this is something you'd return to or find yourself thinking about much but it passes the time and is very likeable. By the way, the Hammer House of Horror episode The Silent Scream would appear to be inspired by this film.

84

THE HOUSE THAT VANISHED (1973)

The House That Vanished (aka Scream – and Die!) was directed by José Ramón Larraz and written by Derek Ford. This is a rather obscure film but one that is not devoid of merit for fans of low-budget British horror. A model named Valerie Jennings (played by Playboy and Penthouse pin-up Andrea Allan) visits a house in the woods with her boyfriend Terry (Alex Leppard). Terry is supposed to be a photographer but it appears he is also a burglar on the side or something. Once inside the house, Valerie witnesses a brutal murder and Terry seems to vanish. Valerie is chased by the killer but manages to elude him in a junkyard.

In the house, Valerie and Terry had found a number of passports belonging to women - which obviously indicated that these were the mementos of a serial killer. When she gets home Valerie finds there is no sign of Terry and that his flat has been burgled. Her friends persuade her not to go to the police in case she is implicated in the burglary and disappearance. Valeries decides to carry on as normal and starts a relationship with a shy artist named Paul (Karl Lanchbury). Valerie is perplexed though by her inability to find the house where she witnessed the murder. What in the name of Giallo is going on?

The House That Vanished is quite enjoyable in parts thanks to its exploitation elements and Italian influences. Parts of this film are not entirely unlike watching a Pete Walker film. I think the main problem with the film is the pacing. After the shocking opening to the film it is a bit sedate and quiet for a good chunk and this might stretch the patience of some viewers. One other problem with parts of this film, and it is something that old low-budget horror films often have in common, is that The House That Vanished
is occasionally so dark you can't actually see what is happening.

And another problem (just one more thing, as Columbo might say) is that The House That Vanished is quite predictable in the end. You won't need to be a genius to work out who the killer is. Still, despite its obvious weaknesses, The House That Vanished is quite good fun at times with some moments of gore and violence and that typically early 70s exploitation aura. The lovely Andrea Allan (who was in stuff like UFO and The Benny Hill Show) is easy on the eye as Valerie and you also get Judy Matheson as her friend. Matheson was no stranger to horror because she came into this film off the back of Lust for a Vampire, Twins of Evil, Crucible of Terror, and The Flesh and Blood Show. Karl Lanchbury, who plays Paul, had a fruitful association with José Ramón Larraz because he was in Deviation and Vampyres.

Peter Forbes-Robertson, who plays the eccentric neighbour Mr Hornby was in all manner of stuff - including Doctor Who and The Tripods. Mr Hornby may or may not be a red herring in the film. You'll just have to watch The House That Vanished and find out for yourself. Maggie Walker, who plays Aunt Susanna, didn't seem to do much acting aside from this and her credits peter out in the mid 1970s. If this was a Pete Walker film than Aunt Susanna would have been played by Sheila Keith I suspect. Edmund Pegge, who plays Kent in the film, has the most impressive CV of anyone in the cast and went on to appear in everything from Tenko to Rosemary & Thyme to The Bill. Pegge also appeared in the Wolf Creek television series based on the two horror films.

The House That Vanished is full of weird details - like the naked woman with a pet monkey and Paul carrying on with his aunt. I like the atmospheric opening to this film, I generally like the cast, and I enjoyed the horror thriller style of the story. The main problems are the pacing and the fact that The House That Vanished is quite predictable in the end. This is nowhere near as good as Symptoms, one of José Ramón Larraz's other British films (we shall discuss Symptoms later on), but it certainly isn't bad for what it is. The House That Vanished is no classic for sure but it is, for the most part anyway, watchable enough with some effective moments of horror and a few twists.

I BOUGHT A VAMPIRE MOTORCYCLE (1990)

I Bought a Vampire Motorcycle was directed by Dirk Campbell. It was written by two Central Television executives - which might explain why this film seems to contain the entire cast of the old ITV show Boon. At the start of the film an occult ritual by a biker gang is violently attacked by another group of bikers. The spirit of evil summoned by the occultists ends up taking refuge in a Norton motorcycle. A motorcycle courier named Noddy (Neil Morrissey) purchases the motorcycle but obviously has no idea this is a demonic bike. It doesn't take too long though for the body count to start piling up. Cue assorted blood drenched killer bike capers in the backstreets of Birmingham...

I Bought a Vampire Motorcycle clearly owes something to the groovy seventies horror film Psychomania with inspiration also coming from possesed vehicle films like Christine, The Car, and Killdozer. Psychomania has some creepiness and trippiness and psychedelia though to go with its daft low-budget horror bike shenanigans and these are three qualities that I Bought a Vampire Motorcycle sorely lacks. The character played by Neil Morrissey in this film would have been played by Robin Askwith or Nicky Henson if they'd made this film in the 1970s. The eccentric Inspector Cleaver played by Michael Elphick in the film feels somewhat patterned on Donald Pleasance in Death Line and Alfred Marks in Scream and Scream Again. Although I like Michael Elphick, his deadpan cartoon reactions to all the murder and mayhem in this film don't really work. The same goes for the character of Noddy. Shown the severed head of his murdered best friend, Noddy shows no reaction and starts cracking lame puns. Even in a horror comedy you have to have one foot in some sort of plausibility.

I Bought a Vampire Motorcycle was apparently influenced by The Evil Dead most of all - a film which the writers of Vampire Motorcycle said was an inspiration because it showed you didn't need much money to make a good horror film. I Bought a Vampire Motorcycle clearly had a meagre budget but it doesn't really matter too much because the practical old school effects are quite good and there is plenty of gore. From a modern vantage point, where low-budget horror films are now blighted by unconvincing CG blood splatters and gore, the old fashioned gore effects in I Bought a Vampire Motorcycle are good fun. I also like the ordinary streets and real locations in this film. I gather they only built one set and shot a lot of stuff outdoors.

The opening to the film with the occult bikers is quite atmospheric and I like the shots of the demon bike in front of a red background - like something out of Creepshow. While this attempt to do a tongue-in-cheek horror film on a shoestring is admirable and even likeable I have one major and not insignificant problem with I Bought a Vampire Motorcycle. The film isn't funny! At all. This is a comedy horror film and I sat stonefaced throughout. I literally didn't laugh once. Over 100 minutes without so much as a titter. The jokes in this film are terrible, the sight gags fall flat on their face, and none of the cast are funny. The film descends (quite literally in one case) into toilet humour and Noddy's sex jokes definitely wouldn't fly today. Neil Morrissey, who a few years later became very famous thanks to the sitcom Men Behaving Badly, is not funny in the least as Noddy. Daniel Peacock (who plays Noddy's friend Buzzer) is probably the cast member here with the best gift for comedy but sadly he disappears far too quickly.

At one point, Burt Kwouk turns up as a Chinese takeaway owner and his shop is called Fu King. That's the sort of jokes you get. An old man keeps being run over in a repeating sight gag. Noddy keeps grabbing the breasts of his girlfriend Kim (Amanda Noar). None of this stuff is funny. My second big problem with I Bought a Vampire Motorcycle is Anthony Daniels. Yes, old C-3PO himself. About half-way through the film Daniels is introduced as a priest who Noddy wants to perform an exorcism on the demon bike. Having watched this film I can now see why Daniels hasn't done much acting outside of Star Wars. Blimey, he is dreadful in this film. The annoying priest character played by Daniels suddenly becomes a giant anchor dragging I Bought a Vampire Motorcycle down below the waves. Daniels goes way over the top and tries to take over the film. His agent probably told him he was the star of I Bought a Vampire Motorcycle.

One other problem, now that I come to think of it, is that I Bought a Vampire Motorcycle is neither scary or creepy either. So you have a horror comedy that isn't funny and isn't scary. The one saving grace is the gore and the demon bike antics. These elements of the film are likeable and pretty good fun at times. There are decapitations, people lose hands and fingers, and a nurse (played by Grange Hill star Paula Ann Bland) is cut in two in a hospital. The film is very watchable and quite likeable early on but runs out of (ahem) mileage somewhere along the line and even the demon bike carnage starts to become repetitive and boring in the end. Now, this is not to say I Bought a Vampire Motorcycle is not worth watching because it's worth a look for the practical gore effects alone. This film essentially tries to bring back the sort of daft horror film made in Britain in the 1970s and for that can only be applauded. I admire the plucky spirit of I Bought a Vampire Motorcycle but I just wish the film had been funnier and scarier.

I DON'T WANT TO BE BORN (1975)

Poor old Joan Collins. She really did hate that fallow middle part of her career where she had to appear in some horror films in order to pay the gas bill and put food on the table. Joan was not a big horror fan but needs must. Out of the horror films she made, 1975's I Don't Want to Be Born (aka The Devil Within Her and Sharon's Baby) is definitely one she'd probably like to forget. This film was directed by Peter Sasdy - who directed some Hammer pictures and the excellent The Stone Tape for television. The screenplay was by Stanley Price. I Don't Want to Be Born was accused of ripping off The Exorcist and Rosemary's Baby but the weird thing about the film is the way it anticipates The Omen (which came out a year later). The plot of I Don't Want to Be Born begins with Lucy (Joan Collins) working in a grotty strip club. In her dressing room, Lucy spurns a lecherous advance from Hercules (George Claydon), the dwarf who is part of her stage act. Joan Collins is definitely a bit on the posh side to be a believable stripper if you ask me and why is there a dwarf as part of her act? I have no idea.

Anyway, Hercules is furious when Lucy gives him the brush off but then becomes amorous with the manager Tommy (John Steiner). Hercules notices this and afterwards confronts Lucy with warnings of a curse. "You will have a baby ... a monster! As big as I am small and possessed by the devil himself!" We now cut to months later. Lucy is no longer a stripper and has gone up in the world. She is married to wealthy Italian businessman Gino Carlesi (Ralph Bates) and lives in a plush gaff in London. She is also pregnant and Lucy and Gino are - after a painful delivery - delighted to welcome a boy into the world. However, the happiness is short lived because the baby seems to take a dislike to Lucy and is unusually large and strong. A number of strange events occur. The baby demolishes its room, torments the housekeeper Mrs Hyde (Hilary Mason), punches people in the face (from its cot!), tries to drown the nurse Jill Fletcher (Janet Key), and so on. This is merely the tip of the infant mayhem iceberg this satanic baby unleashes on Mr and Mrs Carlesi. Soon their very lives are under threat. Will our long suffering heroine Lucy manage to break the curse plaguing this monstrous child?

I Don't Want to Be Born is a pretty terrible film but it does have its rewards. There is a memorable decapitation scene (which again anticipates The Omen) and also an effective sequence where Gino becomes under threat of being hanged in the garden. Ralph Bates is unwittingly hilarious in this film because he has the worst Italian accent ever put on film. Chico Marx was a more convincing Italian than Ralph Bates is in I Don't Want to Be Born. At the start of the film I thought Ralph's character was supposed to be English but just doing a risible Italian accent as a joke to make his wife laugh. Then the penny dropped that Ralph REALLY is supposed to be Italian and would be lumbered with this preposterous accent for the rest of the film. I suppose him being called Gino really should have tipped me off.

Another highlight of this film is Donald Pleasence as Dr Finch. Donald Pleasence could be sympathetic, he could be a villain, he could be funny, he could be stark raving bonkers. In this film though he plays his role completely straight and it is perfect because it makes him seem like a real doctor! This is a very daft film so Pleasence supplies some much needed gravitas and calmness. Eileen Atkins plays Gino's sister Albana - who very conveniently for plot purposes happens to be a nun. Eileen Atkins is far too good for this nonsense - as is Hilary Mason as the housekeeper Mrs Hyde. Mason had fairly recently come off her role as the blind psychic Heather in Nicolas Roeg's Don't Look Now. The legendary Caroline Munro is also in the film as Lucy's friend Mandy. It is very obvious though (too obvious in fact) that Caroline Munro's dialogue has all been dubbed by another actress (Liz Fraser apparently). By this stage of her career the penny must have dropped for Caroline that she wasn't being hired for her acting.

John Steiner is great in this film as Lucy's sleazy former strip club manager Tommy. Lucy tracks Tommy down because she thinks he might be the baby's father. Tommy gets a punch in the mush from the baby for his trouble when they meet - which amuses Lucy no end. George Claydon, who plays Hercules, was an Oompa Loompa in Willy Wonka & the Chocolate Factory and also in Berserk! with Joan Crawford. I'm not sure if you could have an actor with dwarfism as a grotesque villain today. There weren't roles like Tyrion Lannister in Game of Thrones knocking around in George's day. Look out by the way for Floella Benjamin (now Baroness Floella Benjamin OBE) as a nurse. Her part in this film would have been shortly before Floella became a presenter on the beloved children's show Play School. Stanley Lebor, best known as Howard in Ever Decreasing Circles but in everything from Flash Gordon to Minder, also pops up as a police officer.

I Don't Want to Be Born is one of those films that is so bad it becomes quite entertaining. One of the most ludicrous aspects to the film is that we are constantly told that Lucy's baby is unusually large and giant sized for a baby and yet whenever we see the baby it is clearly just a normal sized average infant. As soon as Gino's nun sister is introduced you JUST know we are going to get a hokey exorcism sequence and sure enough this eventually transpires. One thing that is quite enjoyable about the film is the extensive outdoor location work - so extensive in fact that some of it feels suspiciously designed to pad out the running length of the film. From a modern vantage point though it's fun to get these authentic snapshots of London in 1974/75.

I Don't Want to Be Born is laughably awful but builds to an entertaining climax with the murderous baby carnage escalating all the time. Add in an eccentric score by Ron Grainer and you are left with a film that none of the cast were especially happy to have on their CV but is certainly good for a few laughs to any British horror completist who hasn't got around to this yet.

INCENSE FOR THE DAMNED (1971)

Incense for the Damned (aka Bloodsuckers) was directed by Robert Hartford-Davis - though he had his name taken off this film because he was so unhappy with it. There are a couple of other Robert Hartford-Davis films in this book and both of them are a lot more entertaining than this one. Incense for the Damned is one of the worst films I have ever sat through in my life. This film suffered a lot of production problems and was shut down at one point due to lack of funding. When some new funding was secured and they resumed shooting they had to use a few different actors and change the script. This would probably explain why Incense for the Damned, despite being based on the book Doctors Wear Scarlet by Simon Raven, doesn't make much sense.

The story revolves around Richard Fountain (Patrick Mower), a young hotshot don at Oxford who went missing while researching a book in Greece. A foreign office chap named Seymour (Alexander Davion) and Fountain's girlfriend (Madeleine Hinde) and friend (Johnny Sekka) head for Greece to look for him. It transpires that Fountain has fallen under the spell of a vampire cult led by a woman named Chriseis (Imogen Hassall). It will be a pesky task indeed to extract Fountain and bring him home...

The plot synopsis for Incense for the Damned makes this film sound considerably more entertaining than it is to actually watch. I would certainly lower those expectations to when it comes to vampire shenanigans in this film. There is literally about two minutes of vampire stuff in a running time which comes in at just under ninety minutes. Most of the film concerns the trio looking for Richard Fountain in Greece and they are joined by Patrick Macnee as the British military attaché Maj. Derek Longbow. Oh, and Fountain's mentor and potential father in law at Oxford is played by Peter Cushing. Plus you get Edward Woodward as Dr Halstrom, an expert in vampirism.

Blimey, you must be thinking, what a great cast. Patrick Macnee, Peter Cushing, and Edward Woodward. Sadly though though Cushing is barely in the film, Woodward has little more than a cameo, and Patrick Macnee phones in his performance as if he's on holiday - which in a sense he was I suppose. At the very least he had a nice time shooting this film in Greece and Cyprus. There's a lot of narration in the film in a futile attempt to make the story seem coherent and plenty of travelogue shots of Greece which are nice at first but quickly become boring. You can at least give them credit though for real locations.

Patrick Mower spends much of the film in a vacant haze as Fountain and then when he finally does get to speak at the end and is given a big dramatic speech he is absolutely terrible. If they had the Razzies in 1971 I think old Patrick might have been in contention. A gyrating Imogen Hassall tries hard as the sultry Chriseis but isn't in the film enough to really register. Incense for the Damned seems quite tame compared to some of the other films of Robert Hartford-Davis although it does have a psychedelic orgy sequence that goes on for several minutes. The problem is though that if you've seen one psychedelic orgy sequence you've seen them all and so having a bunch of naked people writing around in a drug induced haze to weird flashing lights quickly becomes boring and makes your finger instinctively loom longingly over the fast forward button.

Much of the film plays like a tedious espionage caper as the authorities and Fountain's friends try to work out where he is and what has happened to him. This is punctuated by a number of lightweight cartoon fights and punch-ups which, with the inappropriately jazzy score and fondness for random close ups, makes it often feel as if you are watching one of those cheapjack ITC shows like The Champions or The Adventurer - although you'd probably have a lot more fun watching The Champions than you would Incense for the Damned.

It's a shame really that this film is such a mess because it does waste some very famous actors. Edward Woodward is the highlight for me as Dr Halstrom, who explains (with some relish), that vampirism is a sexual perversion if you ask him (and the government is asking him in this specific case). I would happily have watched an entire film of
Dr Halstrom investigating vampires but sadly no such film transpires.

The Senegalese born actor Johnny Sekka (who served in the RAF and based himself in England after attending RADA) is more or less the male lead in this film, or close to it at least, as Bob Kirby. This makes Incense for the Damned fairly novel for a British film of this era to have a black actor in such a prominent role and playing a hero too. Peter Cushing plays D. Walter Goodrich, the Provost of (the fictional) Lancaster College. Cushing only has a few scenes so I'd imagine he shot his contribution quite quickly. I wouldn't be surprised if they booked Peter for a single day. Incense for the Damned is a terrible film that doesn't work on any level and is a complete mess. The basic idea of the film (young don falls into the clutches of a louche vampire cult) is quite good but but it goes nowhere with that idea and our characters ambling around in Greece soon becomes tiresome. You probably have no good reason to ever watch Incense for the Damned - aside perhaps from Edward Woodward's brief appearance and Imogen Hassall belly dancing.

INSEMINOID (1981)

Inseminoid is a sci-fi horror film directed by the cultish Norman J. Warren. You wouldn't say Inseminoid is forgotten or obscure as I've seen it on television more than once but the film is not THAT famous outside cult horror circles. Inseminoid is probably best known for its amazing poster. The main difference between Norman J. Warren and Pete Walker is that

Walker's films were set in the real world with human villains whereas Warren was more willing to embrace things like the supernatural and science fiction. Inseminoid is often dubbed an Alien copycat - although the makers insist it was written (Inseminoid was written by Nick and Gloria Male) and greenlit before Alien even came out. Norman J. Warren said he'd never even watched Alien when he made this film.

"They agreed it was not an Alien rip-off, and in fact, the head of Fox sent us a very nice letter saying how much he enjoyed the film and wished us luck with the release," said Warren on the similarities. "I find it flattering that anyone can compare Alien, which cost in the region of $30 million, with Inseminoid which cost less than £1 million. We must have done something right." Whatever the truth there are some obvious similarities between the two films. The key difference is that Alien, as Warren pointed out, is an expensive and well made film while Inseminoid was shot in four weeks in some caves. The premise of Inseminoid has a team of astronaut scientists conducting an archaeological excavation on the ruins of an ancient alien civilisation. They meddle with some crystals and awaken something nasty. A crazed Sandy (Judy Geeson) is given some sort of artificial insemination by the aliens and starts bumping off the rest of the scientists to protect her alien offspring.

There is a Roger Corman quality to Inseminoid and the film it sort of resembles is Corman's Galaxy of Terror. But Galaxy of Terror had a young James Cameron working on the designs and special effects and is quite well made for a film of its type and budget. Inseminoid is sometimes jarringly amateurish and bargain basement and doesn't make an awful lot of sense. It has a little notoriety though, mainly thanks to an alien rape scene involving the wholesome Judy Geeson. I have a sweet tooth for these B movie Alien inspired films like Galaxy of Terror, Forbidden World, Creature (aka The Titan Find), and The Intruder Within and Inseminoid sort of fits into this genre. Inseminoid is a very cold and aloof and unpleasant sort of film though that isn't easy to love. The electronic score by John Scott in Inseminoid is very good and to be fair to the film it does have a good atmosphere due to being set in alien caves. The opening to the film with two astronauts in the caves is well done and draws us in. Inseminoid wisely avoids any spaceship stuff because that would have been rough given the budget.

Chislehurst Caves, where this film was shot (caves were used to save money as it would be expensive to build cave sets in a studio), is a twenty-two mile stretch of caves and caverns in Bromley. I'm always fascinated by films made or set in caves. Now, most of them aren't very good (Alien 2: On Earth, What Waits Below etc) but you have had some crackers like The Descent, My Bloody Valentine and George Romero's Day of the Dead. In the vast middle ground you have things like The Strangeness - which is amateurish and rubbish but sort of fun. Inseminoid is a cut above stuff like The Strangeness and Alien 2: On Earth but never quite becomes as much fun or as satisfying as you want it to be. The alien civilisation stuff in Inseminoid is frustratingly vague and the alien puppets (Fraggle Rock via a bad acid trip) are not very good.

Inseminoid is a pretty sleazy entry in the crowded sci-fi horror genre with plenty of rape symbolism. The film's obsession with birth and motherhood is not something I was especially interested in or needed. It wouldn't have bothered me if they had simply gone for more a straight ahead alien monster on the loose sort of film. They had the perfect constrictive location for that type of story. The artificial insemination and birth sequences are hardly tasteful, though fans of Warren might enjoy the exploitation nature of the film. There is plenty of gore too throughout though. Victoria Tennant is taken out with a pair of scissors! At one point a character traps their foot in some rocks and decides (as you do) that the obvious solution to this problem is to saw their own foot off. Rather than have a monster on the loose, the antagonist becomes a feral alien possessed Judy Geeson - which is different I suppose.

Stephanie Beacham is the most competent actress on show (notice how they get Beacham to deliver the opening exposition) in a largely no name cast. Beacham radiates a polite indifference to the whole affair. She knows this film isn't up to much but she has bills to pay and a baby to feed. To be fair, Judy Geeson is game and throws herself into the most infamous part she was ever likely to play. Look out for Robert Pugh in this film by the way. He later played Craster in Game of Thrones. Rosalind Lloyd, who plays Gail in this film, played the wife of Lewis Collins in Who Dares Wins. She was later in the Fools and Horses episode Diamonds Are for Heather. The characters in the film are not that interesting and read their lines flatly as if they are eager to get this over with (given that the cast were in damp dusty caves this was understandable).

Inseminoid did a couple of days shooting in a rocky part of Malta in order to depict the surface of the planet. They put these location shots through a red filter in the film.

The cave location gives Inseminoid a nice strange atmosphere but the effects, props, costumes, and performances are average for even a cheapie exploitation film. Case in point - motorcycle crash helmets are deployed for the astronaut helmets. Inseminoid seems to have a few fans out there but it's easy to see why this horror film hasn't really stood the test of time. There are better Alien copycats out there if you are into that. I find Inseminoid quite interesting and I always give it another go if I stumble across it on television but this is one of those films that I want to like much more than I ever actually do. By the way, at the end of this film a couple of space soldiers with guns turn up to investigate what has happened at the base. This sort of anticipates James Cameron's Aliens a bit doesn't it?

KILLER'S MOON (1978)

Killer's Moon was written and directed by Alan Birkinshaw.

This film is sometimes dubbed a British version of I Spit On Your Grave and has been called the nastiest and sleaziest film ever coughed up by the British film industry. That's probably not quite the case - though you can see why this film is never on the telly. It isn't the gore drenched slasher it is sometimes portrayed as being but it is rather tasteless at the best of times. Killer's Moon is sort of like a mash up of A Clockwork Orange, an episode of Please Sir!, and the 1974 American exploitation film Carnal Madness.

A coach carrying schoolgirls breaks down in the Lake District and so along with their two female teachers they set off on foot and find an empty remote woodland hotel that isn't open yet. The hotel keeper decides to take them in anyway but the phone line goes dead. It turns out that roaming in the countryside outside are four violent and disturbed escaped lunatics who were part of an LSD experiment in which they carried out their darkest desires in controlled dreams. The lunatics think they are still dreaming and are unaware that the hotel and schoolgirls are actually real. Well, you can see where this is heading can't you?

Killer's Moon begins with the coach conking out in a little village. It's a bit like watching Last of the Summer Wine at first - especially with the broad comic performance by the coach driver (played by a real life comedian named Chubby Oates). The schoolgirls, as you would expect, are suspiciously mature and look more like Benny Hill's backing dancers than real schoolgirls. The actors playing the schoolgirls are a trifle wooden but generally not as bad as you might fear. JoAnne Good, who plays Mary, is now a famous radio presenter and was in everything from Only Fools and Horses to The Bill. Lisa Vanderpump, who plays the schoolgirl Anne, is actually a famous reality television star in America these days and was in The Real Housewives of Beverly Hills.

Anyway, the early schoolgirl scenes are not actually that bad.

Alan Birkinshaw's sister Fay Weldon had a hand in the script (which she apparently regretted when she saw the film) and it is in these early scenes which try to flesh out the schoolgirl characters a bit where you can detect the influence of Weldon. Where you don't detect the influence of Weldon is in the rest of the film. Well, not unless she decided that Killer's Moon needed more rape, axe murders, nudity, and schoolgirls being strangled. The schoolgirls are aided by Pete (Anthony Forrest) and Mike (Tom Marshall), two young men who are camping in the area. These two characters are played by the worst actors you've ever seen in your life and so quickly become annoying. You start to dread the regular visits to their tent. Mike is so chipper and unfussed by any of the carnage happening in the film that he can't help but dissipate some of the tension Killer's Moon is groping for. There is also a three legged dog who becomes a hero and a flinty Scottish gamekeeper who disappears far too quickly.

Mr Smith (Nigel Gregory), Mr Trubshaw (David Jackson), Mr Muldoon (Paul Rattee) and Mr Jones (Peter Sprag) are the four escaped lunatics who arrive at the hotel to terrify the girls. They are dressed like droogs from A Clockwork Orange and waste no time in raping one of the schoolgirls. The four lunatics are not especially scary and they become quite irritating in the end because they never stop talking and the actors playing them give very unrestrained hammy performances. It might have worked better if the lunatics had been more mysterious and in the shadows. The only one of the lunatic actors I recognised was David Jackson - who I recall from a couple of episodes of Minder. There are no stars in the film but people you'll recognise from other things. Elizabeth Counsell, who plays Miss Lilac, was in the sitcom Brush Strokes and Hilda Braid, who plays the hotel keeper, was Nana Moon in EastEnders and appearing in the sitcom Citizen Smith around the time Killer's Moon was shot.

A framing sequence involving government bigwigs tells us that these violent patients escaped not from a 'loony bin' (as one of the schoolgirls puts it) but a cottage hospital! I have a cottage hospital at the end of my street and all this time I thought it was just somewhere you went if you got a bad cut. I had no idea that violent psychopaths underwent LSD experiments in these places. I'm definitely locking my back door tonight. Suffice to say, this film is rife with bizarre tangents like this. The school bus is supposed to be on the way to Scotland so why is it on some tiny woodland road? Why not just go on the main road and motorway?

And also, why is there not a single police officer searching for the escaped lunatics? Surely the area would be crawling with police search teams, sniffer dogs, and probably a helicopter. I suppose you aren't supposed to scrutinise films like this for logic and I suspect the cottage hospital was only included to set up a joke about the NHS which one of the escapees delivers. One other common nit-pick about this film is the bungled 'day for night' shooting - which is inconsistent to say the least. What are the positives of Killer's Moon? Armathwaite Hall (a luxury hotel adjacent to Bassenthwaite Lake) was used in the film and it makes a fine spooky location in the gloom and mist. The central idea, while daft, is also quite clever and interesting. The notion that these men think they are dreaming so can do whatever they want with no consequences. At one point one of the lunatics ponders whether he is in his own dream or someone else's dream.

The strangulation sequence in the lake is quite striking and rather chilling too. It's one of the few moments in the film where Birkinshaw seems to nail what he was aiming for - a low-budget trashy horror film with a bit of art to it. I think people tend to go into Killer's Moon expecting a notorious blood gushing slasher film and if you are expecting that you are likely to be disappointed. The film is quite slow and never as lean or tense as it should be. Killer's Moon is definitely unpleasant at times (the rape sequence) and I really did not care for the scene where where one of the lunatics is cruel to a cat. I have cats myself so, as you might imagine, this hit a very raw spot for me. Leave the cats out of these films please. There are some gnarly deaths in the film but you've probably seen a lot worse when it comes to gore and sadism. Killer's Moon looks like Last of the Summer Wine compared to modern horror films like Terrifier 2.

The most infamous and jaw dropping moment in Killer's Moon comes when one of the schoolgirls tries to console another and says that rape isn't that bad and if she keeps it secret she can still be a wife and mother one day. I'd lay down good money this wasn't one of Fay Weldon's contributions to the script. Killer's Moon is definitely an odd film. It's like they took St Trinians, a Carry On film, and A Clockwork Orange and blended it with a tasteless exploitation horror film. Killer's Moon isn't anywhere near as competent, well acted, and coherent as the modestly budgeted British horror films Peter Walker was making in this decade but if nothing else it is an experience.

LIGHTHOUSE (1999)

Lighthouse was directed by Simon Hunter. This film sat on the shelf for a while but then got a theatrical release. In the United States it was called Dead of Night. How original! Lighthouse was something I'd never heard of until recently so when I learned of a late 1990s British slasher film set in a lighthouse my curiosity was piqued. Having watched the film I can now see why Lighthouse is so obscure. This plays a lot like an early 2000s straight to DVD film or one of those dismal modern British horror films you start watching on the old Horror Channel but tap out of after about half an hour. The film begins with a ramshackle ship in rough seas transporting a bunch of prisoners to a prison island. This is a very ludicrous start to the film. Why not use a helicopter? The prisoners are manacled down below and a bunch of suited prison officers watch over them. These include Don Warrington. Don, bless him, gives by far the worst performance in the film.

The film opens with a black and white montage of Rachel Shelley as psychologist Dr Kirsty McCloud typing her report on a notorious serial killer named Leo Rock (Christopher Adamson). Leo keeps the heads of his victims as trophies. Well, Leo is a captive on this prison ship too. Dr Kirsty McCloud is on the ship also for reasons which remain slightly vague. I probably won't be ruining anything by telling you that the serial killer maniac Leo escapes and makes his way to a lighthouse situated (as lighthouses tend to be) on some craggy rocks. Leo kills the men in the lighthouse and, meanwhile, the prison ship hits a rock and starts sinking. They really didn't think through this transporting prisoners in a rusty old ship business did they? A small group of prisoners and prison officers make it ashore to the lighthouse - where Leo Rock is waiting to murder them all. They must all work together if they are to have any hope of survival.

Lighthouse (which owes something to Tower of Evil - a film we will get to later in the book) has a pretty good premise for a horror film but I can't say I found the end result hugely entertaining. The dialogue and acting in this film is atrocious and the characters are vague and ill defined. The odd thing about this film is how much it seems to be influenced by Alien 3. Lighthouse seeks to mimic Alien 3 with a gritty bleak rain sodden aura and convicts having to battle a fearsome terror. This is where the comparisons end because Alien 3, whatever its flaws (and Alien 3 has PLENTY of flaws), was a big budget film with a great cast directed by David Fincher. Lighthouse does not have a big budget nor a great cast and it definitely wasn't directed by David Fincher.

The main lead here is James Purefoy as a convict named Spader. If this was an old John Carpenter film, Spader would be played by Kurt Russell but sadly this isn't an old John Carpenter film. Purefoy's character, like the others is ill defined. Spader is not exactly Napoleon Wilson or Riddick in Pitch Black. Purefoy tries to do the cool anti-hero thing but it doesn't really work. I think a problem with Lighthouse is that you never buy into the premise of the film and you never buy into these characters. It all feels so contrived and hollow. There is one great scene in Lighthouse though where a character hides in a rowing boat on the beach and the killer Leo places the heads of his victims on top of the boat. The man hiding has to stay quiet and blood starts to drip from the heads onto his face. Tense scenes like this are a little oasis of what is largely a desert of mediocre horror tedium.

There's another decent scene where Captain Campbell (Paul Brooke) has to hide in a toilet while the killer lurks outside. The film doesn't have enough of this though and too often consists of people shouting at each other and scenes outside which are so dark you can barely see anything. The film hints (more than hints really) at a connection between Leo Rock and Dr Kirsty McCloud but never really goes anywhere with this. I can't say I found Leo Rock very scary in this film. He's no threat to Michael Myers or Jason. He's just basically a bloke with a grease back who walks very slowly. You could probably stop to run a bath if he was chasing you.

There's a bit of gore in the film but nothing to write home about. The last two characters left standing at the end will come as no surprise so Lighthouse doesn't really subvert any of your expectations. Lighthouse is the sort of thing that a prime Neil Marshall (circa 2005) probably could have made fun and memorable and there was definitely potential in the story. Despite a few moments of promise here and there, Lighthouse is very forgettable on the whole and (no pun intended) awash with bad acting and terrible dialogue. This is one of those horror films that becomes something of a slog long before the running time is over.

LINK (1986)

Link was directed by Richard Franklin and written by Everett De Roche. The film features Terence Stamp and Elisabeth Shue but the best acting performance in the film is by an orangutan. This is nothing new in cinema. Just ask Clint Eastwood. Richard Franklin's stock was very high when he made this film thanks to things like Patrick, Psycho II, and Roadgames. Link did not do very well though and seems to have been largely forgotten these days. This is definitely a very strange film and I couldn't really tell you what made Franklin determined to make a killer monkey caper. He said he was inspired by films like The Birds and was interested when he read about how chimps have tribal conflicts and civil wars with one another in some circumstances. I don't know what these monkey civil wars are over. It could be bananas presumably.

In the film, Elisabeth Shue plays a young zoology student who takes a summer job at a remote home on the English coast with Dr Steven Phillip (Terence Stamp). Dr Phillip is an anthropologist studying the intelligence of chimpanzees. The house is full of various chimps and the biggest character is the cigar smoking chimp Locke. At some point, Dr Phillip seems to vanish. Jenny presumes he has gone to London and stays on in the house with the chimps. However, the chimps begin to get fractious and Jenny realises she might be in danger...

I can't say that animals in horror films are my favourite thing and Link doesn't really do too much to alter this stance. The film is somewhat like watching a family comedy with funny chimps at first (especially with the music by Jerry Goldsmith) but then becomes crazier and crazier until it ends up as something akin to a slasher film - only with a chimp as the maniac rather than a human. Locke the chimp in this film is so intelligent he becomes like Jason Bourne in the end as he outsmarts the humans. The film is quite tense in places and does have a memorably preposterous death by letter box with an obviously fake monkey paw snaking through to pull some poor blighter into the door.

A few years after this film came out, George Romero made a monkey themed horror thriller called Monkey Shines. I have no idea what possessed genre greats like Franklin and George Romero to make chimp themed horror films. Out of the two films I'd say that Link is a bit more stupidly entertaining than Monkey Shines but Monkey Shines has more interesting ideas and is a better film than Link. I personally won't be rushing back to either of them in a hurry though. The main chimp in Link was actually an orangutan in real life. They just disguised the orangutan and darkened it. They should have a new category at the Oscars - Best Performance By An Orangutan Playing A Chimpanzee. I don't know if Locke the orangutan was a method actor and spent a few months living as a chimp in preparation for Link.

Locke is great in the film though and steals the show although Elisabeth Shue is good too. I don't suppose this film did too much for Shue's career at the time but she was back on her feet not long after with things like Adventures in Babysitting and the Back to the Future sequels. Terence Stamp gives an eccentric performance that is not without its charms. Just between you and me, I don't think Terence is taking this film too seriously. It was probably just a quick cheque to him. I can picture Stamp phoning his agent and asking if the money from the monkey film has gone into the bank yet. There's no information online about how much money Locke was paid for the film but you'd guess that he didn't get quite as much money as Terence Stamp. Locke also negotiated a bonus. If the film earned a certain profit he got some monkey nuts.

Richard Franklin apparently came under pressure from the studio to use actors in ape suits (Greystoke style) rather than real chimps but he stood his ground and insisted on real animals in the end. This was a sensible idea because Link is a daft film but it would have been dafter still with actors in ape suits running around and you would have lost the great performance of the orangutan. These days a film like this would have CGI chimps - which might look technically impressive but never quite make us suspend our disbelief.

Link has occasionally threatened to become a mild cult film due to its preposterous premise and chimp themed suspense but I can't say it appealed to me an awful lot. Horror fans might be disappointed by the lack of blood and murder (though you get a few) and I really didn't enjoy the scene where a chimp batters and swings a dog like something out of a wrestling match. The locations in this film (which was made in Scotland I believe) are great but this is a film I could take or leave and in the end and would prefer to leave if it's all the same to you. The youngsters who turn up in the film later looking for Jane don't add much to the acting quality but are amusingly dated from a modern perspective. By the way, look out for Tosh Lines from The Bill (Kevin Lloyd) in this film. That's his second mention in this book.

MUMSY, NANNY, SONNY, GIRLY (1970)

Mumsy, Nanny, Sonny and Girly (aka 'Girly') was directed by Freddie Francis and written by Brian Compton. The film is based on a stage play by Maisie Mosco entitled Happy Family. Although this film is rather obscure, Francis considered it to be his best work as a director (this is one of the few films that Francis had complete creative control over - which might explain why he was so fond of it). This is a bizarre horror black comedy and quite possibly a brilliant one too. The film takes place at a grand sprawling country mansion where a family have retreated in a strange old fashioned fantasy world apparently based on children's books. The family are Mumsy

(Ursula Howells), Nanny (Pat Heywood), and the children Sonny (Howard Trevor) and Girly (Vanessa Howard).

Although Sonny and Girly wear school uniforms and are treated like children they look rather on the mature side for such treatment. The family play something they call the 'Game'. This involves luring men back to the house - the men then indoctrinated into the rules of the house and forced to behave like children too. If they don't obey the rules they are 'sent to the angels' - in other words they are killed. Whenever a 'friend' is killed, Sonny records it on a camera and they watch the murder on a projector.

This is the sort of film that is better watched than described. It's a strange film but a very compelling one. The tension arises when a man played by Michael Bryant arrives at the house after Sonny and Girly kill his companion (played by Imogen Hassel) in a park by grabbing her foot when she is on top of a slide in a playground. Bryant goes with them to the house to lay low and is blackmailed because they have the body of the woman in the house. However, Bryant's character observes the family and their bizarre game and concludes that the key to his survival is to get close to Girly. This will create a fracture in the family as Girly won't want to 'share' her new friend - especially when he awakens her sexuality.

This is a beautiful looking film (shot at Oakley Court) and amusingly bizarre and deadpan. I gather that Francis was specifically looking for a film he could shoot at Oakley Court and this film was perfect. It makes a wonderful isolated and anachronistic location for this weird family to lurk around in. There are some good performances in the film but the star is unquestionably Vanessa Howard as Girly. Vanessa Howard is fantastically arch and charismatic and gives a brilliant performance. Vanessa Howard is plainly a star in the making in this film. She has comic charisma to spare and the camera loves her. The tragedy of this film's failure to find an audience, and the subsequent failure of the Amicus film What Became of Jack and Jill?, was that Howard abandoned acting soon afterwards. A terrific shame. Vanessa Howard had no more acting credits after 1973 and moved to the United States, where she married a film producer (Robert Chartoff - who produced the Rocky films) and concentrated on family life.

Mumsy, Nanny, Sonny and Girly bore the brunt of a moral backlash in Blighty due to a scene early on which implies that incest is going on with Girly and Sonny (who are brother and sister). As a consequence of this, few cinemas wanted to show the film. In the United States the title was changed to 'Girly' and the promotional art was focused on Vanessa Howard in her school uniform (Howard was actually twenty-two when she made this film so it isn't as if she was a real schoolgirl). This tactic worked and the film did quite well in the United States and got some decent reviews. Sadly though, Vanessa Howard was apparently oblivious to this and had no idea the film found a modest audience over there. One nice (if bittersweet) addition to this tale is that an event was held at Oakley Court in 2015 to celebrate the film and a memorial bench to Vanessa Howard (who sadly passed away in 2010) was opened there.

Ursula Howells and Pat Heywood are well cast as Mumsy and Nanny although Howard Trevor, who plays the brother of Girly, is something of a liability and clearly can't act. I'm not completely surprised to see that he didn't have any other acting credits after this film. The only other casting complaint you might have is that the rather plain looking Michael Bryant doesn't really seem like the sort of person who would charm and excite Vanessa Howard but then his performance is very good. Mumsy, Nanny, Sonny and Girly is a jet black comedy full of memorable scenes and deadpan wit. Though the film is surreal and darkly comic it does get quite bleak too - like the murder at the start and the scene where the family watch a 'snuff' film of a man hunted on the grounds of the house. This surreal darkness of the premise and the brilliant performance by

Vanessa Howard make this film well worth watching.

THE MUTATIONS (1974)

The Mutations (aka The Mutation, The Freaks, and The Freakmaker) was directed by Jack Cardiff. It was the last film he directed and its failure led him to him going back to being a cinematographer. The Mutations was written by Harold Pinter and adapted from his stage play of the same name. I'm only joking. The film was written by Edward Mann and Robert D. Weinbach. The plot of The Mutations concerns Professor Nolter (Donald Pleasance). Professor Nolter is secretly kidnapping students and crossing them with giant Venus flytraps to create a new race of sentient plant people. Or something like that. Professor Nolter is in desperate need of a hobby if you ask me. He should take up playing bingo. The experiments of Professor Nolter inevitably end up being discarded and handed over to a local circus to use in their freak show.

The Mutations is definitely a strange film. A bit tasteless and exploitative, very silly, but quite watchable all the same and with a good cast. Hammer babe Julie Ege is the heroine as Hedi and the beefy Brad Harris is more or less the male lead as Brian. You don't get too many characters in films named Brian these days do you? There is some spiffy time lapse photography at the start of the film which leads one to expect a more thoughtful and interesting film than the one we get. You could probably describe The Mutations as schlock but that's fine because there is nothing wrong with some retro schlock. Jill Haworth, no stranger to horror at this point of her career, also features in the film as Lauren. The film is quite colourful despite its grim aura and you get a range of locales - from the pristine lab of Nolter to the sawdust of the circus to misty parks to grotty abodes in London.

The Mutations is one of those films where you have no idea what the hell was anyone was thinking when they made it but it does pass the time and certainly isn't boring. If anyone steals this film it is surely the great Tom Baker as Lynch - one of the 'freaks' and Nolter's assistant but not someone who is happy with this situation and aspires to be more than a circus sideshow exhibit. He wants to be cured. Even though he is buried under a lot of makeup and a monstrous mask that unmistakable Tom Baker persona still comes through in spades. He started playing the Doctor in Doctor Who the same year this film came out so you'd imagine he already had the Doctor Who gig in the bag when he did this film. It seems highly unlikely that someone at the BBC was watching The Mutations and when Lynch shuffled into view they suddenly stood up in the cinema and shouted "That's our Doctor!" at the screen.

Donald Pleasance, just as he did in I Don't Want To Be Born, underplays his part in a quiet and unfussy manner. Michael Dunn, a very talented American actor who had dwarfism, plays Burns in the film. Dunn sadly died before The Mutations came out. He passed away in London in 1974 while making a film called The Abdication. Look out by the way for Richard Davies in this film in a small part. He would have been very well known at the time for his fairly recent role in the sitcom Please Sir! as Mr Price. The Mutations is very inspired by Tod Browning's Freaks and even borrows a few scenes and lines from that film. There is a lot of Frankenstein in this film too. The real monster is Professor Nolter - not his experiments. The character in The Mutations who can make his eyes pop out of his head is played by Willie "Popeye" Ingram. Ingram actually worked in real carnival sideshows thanks to his eye bulging antics.

There's quite a lot of circus stuff in the film. Some of it is a bit uncomfortable to watch but most of of it is harmless enough - like a bearded lady for instance. You just knew a bearded lady was going to turn up sooner or later. Professor Nolter has a super ray device in his lab which looks like Auric Goldfinger's laser wotsit that he used when he had Sean Connery strapped to a table in Goldfinger. The device can turn mouldy oranges into fresh oranges. When he demonstrates this to his class the students seem remarkably blasé all things considered as if giant ray devices which can bring rotting fruit back to life are ten a penny and hardly worth waking up for. The last act of the film has a Venus fly trap/human mutation running around and making a nuisance of himself. If this sounds like your cup of tea then you should enjoy The Mutations. This film rarely makes much sense but it is strange, silly, and festooned with familiar faces. No prizes for guessing by the way what happens to Professor Nolter at the end of this film.

OMEN III: THE FINAL CONFLICT (1981)

The third and final Omen sequel (featuring Damien Thorn anyway *) was directed by Graham Baker. The original title of this film was The Final Conflict - the Omen III bit was added later. The Final Conflict was shot in 1979 but sat on the shelf for a couple of years. This film (which was a British co-production) is not exactly obscure but does feel a bit forgotten at times. The Omen was a big blockbuster and I think most people will have some memories of watching Damien - Omen II. Omen II is the one where Damien is at a military academy. I'm actually quite fond of that second film. It has some good elaborate deaths and is pretty good fun. Omen III is definitely a step down from the first two in my opinion. Omen III feels quite drab and lifeless compared to the first two and oddly small scale too. Having said that though, there are fans who think The Final Conflict is underrated and much better than the second one. We all have different likes and dislikes and that's fine.

In the film Damien is now in his thirties and played by Sam Neil. Neil can do the suave thing quite well and looks somewhat sinister but you never get the impression he's really that into this film. Anyway, Damien (like his late father) becomes the American Ambassador to Britain because he has learned that the Second Coming of Christ will occur in England. Naturally, Damien wants to stop this and because that would be bad news for him. However, Father DeCarlo (Rossano Brazzi), a priest from the Subiaco monastery where Father Spiletto spent his final days and observed Damien from afar since his adopted father's death, acquires the Seven Daggers of Megiddo that were dug out of the ruins of the Thorn Museum in Chicago. Joined by six other priests, DeCarlo plans to kill Damien...

Omen III is a bit dull at times and lacks the trashy appeal of the first two films. It's rather predictable and there are a few too many scenes of monks scurrying about in the dark for my liking. Fountains Abbey in Yorkshire was used for these scenes. Don Gordon is pretty good though as Damien's right hand man - although he's clearly not an out and out Satanist because he tries to do a bunk in the end when Damien tells him to kill his own son. Turns out Damien wants to kill all boys born in England on the morning of March 24, 1982 to prevent the Christ Child's return to power. Charming! There don't seem to be as many elaborate tongue-in-cheek Final Destination style deaths in this one although it does have perhaps the most harrowing demise in the trilogy when a priest tries to kill Damien in a television studio and ends up wrapped in burning plastic swinging from the rafters. Nasty.

Lisa Harrow plays Kate, the vague love interest for Damien. Kate is a journalist but Damien is more interested in manipulating her son Peter (Barnaby Holm). The most memorable image in the film comes when Damien arrives by helicopter to address his Satanic disciples on a small island. I think you even see a boy scout amongst the crowd! This scene is quite funny. That's one of the problems with The Final Conflict. It plays straighter than the first two films and so always flirts with being unintentionally funny. It is very dark though in places. Baby deaths, the creepy relationship between Damien and Lisa Harrow's son, and a very brutal suicide of the previous Ambassador at the start. The suicide Ambassador has Ruby Wax as his secretary! Maybe one of the reasons people don't tend to laud Omen III much is the ending. It does feel like a slight cop out to give the Omen trilogy a 'happy' ending. We sort of enjoy Damien being evil and winning don't we?

The continuity of the Omen films does make much sense in that Damien was a little kid in the first film but now five years later in his early thirties. You just have to not worry about stuff like this. I like the location shooting in this film. Plenty of stuff in London and Yorkshire. Damien's house in the film is really Brocket Hall, near Welwyn Garden City, Hertfordshire. The house has been used for many film and television productions including Night of the Demon and Poirot. Hazel Court has a cameo at the fox hunting sequence - during which Damien memorably turns his hounds on one of the priests. The Treffry Viaduct in Cornwall was used for when the man flies off the parapet. Omen III is watchable enough but I don't find it quite as entertaining as the previous two films. It certainly has its moments though.

* Omen IV: The Awakening (1991) was a television film that sought to spin out from the Damien Thorn trilogy of Omen theatrical films. This was directed by Jorge Montesi & Dominique Othenin-Gerard and several people had a hand in the script (never a great sign). The premise has congressman Gene York (Michael Woods) and wife Karen (Faye Grant) adopting a child after they fail to have biological children of their own. The child, a girl named Delia (Asia Vieira plus some child actors of varying ages), turns out to be - wouldn't you know it - bad news. People start to die mysteriously, fires start, Delia acquires a spooky rottweiler, even new age crystals

114

whither and blacken when Delia is around. As ever with the Omen formula, it slowly begins to dawn that there is something of the night about Delia. Will her adopted mother Karen manage to work this out before it's too late?

Omen IV: The Awakening is a very mediocre and lacklustre attempt to wring more mileage out of the Omen brand and doesn't work at all. One of the most salient problems the film grapples with is its obstinate insistence on being a loose remake of the first film. The most obvious mistake of this approach is that - as a television film - it can't use the shock and gore of the original. I need hardly add that it doesn't have Richard Donner, a big budget, and that terrific cast either with Gregory Peck, David Warner et al. Omen IV is bland and flat with an eccentric music score and a preposterous twist at the end that feels like a vague threat that more of these television Omen films might be on the way. Fortunately, that didn't happen in the end. Faye Grant, of V fame, is one of the few familiar faces in the no name cast as the gradually suspecting mother. Grant does her best but Omen IV is a really disappointing and poorly made television thriller for the most part.

PANIC (1978)

Panic is a short film directed by James Dearden. This seventeen minute short was shown before feature films in British cinemas and on television in the United States. It is very highly regarded and a masterclass in tension and suggestion. A woman named Mandy (Julie Neesam) argues with her boyfriend Paul (Peter Blake) about her career as a model. She sets off for work in her car alone. It's a night of torrential rain and she takes pity on an old lady (Avis Bunnage) hitchhiking and picks her up. However, once in the car, Mandy finds the old lady disconcertingly strange and sinister and decides she must come up with a way to dispense with her passenger. And that's just the beginning...

Panic is a great little short and stylishly directed by Deardon (who, sadly it seems, never made a feature film). The film is awash with blue and takes place at night with strobing lights and pounding rain. It looks like a very stylish Italian thriller film despite its very British atmosphere and cast. Avis Bunnage is absolutely terrifying as the hitchhiking old lady. Just one sullen stare from her to Mandy is enough to send a shiver down the spine. No wonder Mandy quickly decides to come up with a ruse to eject her from the car.

This short film has a truly haunting ending that is all the stronger for being slightly suggestive. It is left for us to ponder what will happen next and what has indeed just happened in the first place. The situation it leaves Mandy in at the end is deliciously dark. Panic is essentially the best episode of Hammer House of Mystery & Suspense or Tales of the Unexpected never made. The precise nature of the film is a masterclass considering the brevity of the running time. It tells a complete story with a killer ending and also leaves us with much food for though as we fill in some of the final blanks for ourselves.

British viewers may be amused to see some familiar faces in the cast. Peter Blake played Kirk in the sitcom Dear John while Leonard Fenton, who pops up as a policeman here, was later Dr Legg in the long running soap opera EastEnders. Look out for a young Ray Burdis too. Panic is relatively obscure these days and only seems to exist in rough around the edges form on YouTube. If you like horror anthology episodes and short films then this is not be missed. It packs in more chills and atmosphere in seventeen minutes than most horror films do in two hours.

PAPERHOUSE (1988)

Paperhouse was directed by Bernard Rose (who would go on to

direct Candyman) and written by Matthew Jacobs. The film is based on the book Marianne Dreams by Catherine Storr - which had previously been adapted as the 1972 British ITV children's TV series Escape Into Night. Paperhouse is a dark fantasy children's film - though often categorised as a horror film. Placing this film into a box marked horror is not entirely inappropriate though because it has some scenes which are straight out of a horror film. You could probably call this a sort of children's horror film if you wanted to I suppose. Essentially though this a fantasy drama about a troubled girl who has vivid dreams. I'm amazed to be honest this film is so obscure and is never on television. I love Paperhouse and have no idea why it isn't more famous.

The story revolves an eleven year-old girl named Anna Madden (Charlotte Burke) who is a bit of a tearaway. Anna is the sort of girl who bunks afternoons off school and is gobby in class. She lives with her mother Kate (Glenne Headly) and her father (Ben Cross) seems to be absent a lot due to work. Anna comes down with glandular fever and the doctor (Gemma Jones) orders her to stay in bed until she has recovered. Anna is not too happy about being forced to stay in bed and begins drawing a lot to relieve the boredom. She draws a house and finds that in her dreams she can visit this house. She then draws a boy in the window and the boy now resides in the house when she visits in her dreams. Anna learns though the boy is named Marc (Elliott Spiers) and in the real world is sick in hospital. For some reason Marc is in the real world and in her dreams. Anna attempts to adjust her illustration to make life better for Marc in the dream house but things start to become complicated to say the least.

I gather Paperhouse differs somewhat from the book and previous television adaptation of this story. One new element in this film version introduces is to have Anna's father become an antagonist in the dream world. Anna draws him (she has a special pencil which magically makes things appear in the dream if she draws them but nothing can be erased) looking like a 'madman' by mistake and scribbles over him. In the dreams he now becomes a blind maniac trying to kill Marc. This is the most overt horror section of the film and slightly at odds with the general tone but well done all the same. Anna's father becoming a threat in her dreams suggests some sort of abuse in the real world - and Anna even comments at one point that she doesn't like her dad when he's drunk. The film seems to pull back on this subtext though later on. Anna is initially cold to her father when he returns home but we presume this because she was shaken by the terrible dream (or nightmare really) version of him she encountered with Marc.

Paperhouse doesn't really offer too many explanations for the dream/reality parallels. Given that the link between Anna and Marc is that they have the same doctor we could perhaps offer a hypothesis that the doctor is somehow an unwitting conduit. Maybe the illustration creates a telepathic link. Just think of Anna's pencil as the wardrobe to Narnia or Jamie's magic torch. The film has fun with the fantasy premise of the story. Anna tries to make life better for Marc in the dream house so she draws him an ice cream machine and a bottle of coke. When she visits him in his dreams we see the bottle of coke is huge because her perspective was somewhat wonky. I like the way Anna's illustrations are scribbly and childlike. They don't have her as some genius artist. I have to admit that Paperhouse got me in the 'feels' a couple of times. In its best moments this is a very moving film about trauma, childhood, fears, dreams, nightmares, and life and death. Anna is on the cusp of puberty and this is plainly a factor in her dreams and the imagery of the film.

I've seen in some reviews of Paperhouse the performance by Charlotte Burke as Anna cited as a weak link. This is insanity if you ask me. Charlotte Burke is quite unlike any child actor I've ever seen. Her character is stroppy but still strangely likeable and she sort of deadpans her part and underplays it. Burke conveys both intelligence and a dry sense of humour as Anna and you couldn't imagine anyone else playing this part. This was Charlotte Burke's first and last acting role. She never acted again - which is a shame. Her explanation for why she stopped acting is actually quite touching. Charlotte Burke said she loved Paperhouse so much that she didn't want to be associated with anything else. She wanted Paperhouse to be her only credit.

If this film has an acting blip it is Glenne Headly as Anna's mother. Headly, who is American, had to do her dialogue again through ADR when they decided they wanted Anna's mother to be English. You can tell that Anna's mother is dubbed in the film - albeit dubbed by the same actor. Elliott Spiers is likeable as Marc and has a believable rapport with Charlotte Burke in the film. Paperhouse is even more poignant with the knowledge that Elliott Spiers tragically died in 1994 at the age of twenty. Sadly, I believe he had an adverse reaction to some medication. Most of the film takes place in the London flat of Anna and her mother but you get seaside scenes in Devon and at Highgate High Level station. The scenes of Anna and Marc at the dream house are well designed and the shots of Anna running across empty fields to the house are magical in their own strange way.

You could argue that Paperhouse goes on for slightly longer than it needed to. This is one of those films where you think it has ended up a couple of times but instead it then carries on for another ten minutes. They probably could have tided up the last act a little bit. I do love the film though. Paperhouse is one of those films where you can read it in different ways and come up with your own theories. This is a beautifully made film which lingers in the memory after you've watched it. It should be way more famous but for some reason it bombed and few people ever watched it. Happily though, people are now discovering Paperhouse and watching it for the first time. By the way, the lovely music in the film features early work by Hans Zimmer.

PERSECUTION (1974)

Persecution (aka The Terror of Sheba and The Graveyard) was directed by Don Chaffey. This is a daft thriller in which Lana Turner, in one of her later roles, plays Carrie Masters, a cat obsessed woman living in a country mansion who has always tormented her son David (Ralph Bates). When he returns home as an adult with his wife Janie (Suzan Farmer), Carrie is determined to ruin things for him. How much can David take before he cracks? There are, as you might have guessed, some very dark secrets in this family which will inevitably all be revealed by the end of the film...

Lana Turner called Persecution the worst film she had ever been in and Trevor Howard, who has a couple of scenes in Persecution as Paul Bellamy, also called this a terrible film. Persecution is not THAT bad, it isn't Plan 9 From Outer Space or Carry on Columbus, but by the same token it isn't very good either. This drab and depressing film was made at Pinewood with some exterior location work in Denham. Most of the film takes place in the dark mansion where Lana Turner swans around in regal outfits and is (ahem) catty to her son. Lana Turner's career was obviously in decline by this point. She was now doing television and cheap horror films like this. You could imagine Bette Davis having fun with the part of Carrie Masters but Lana Turner gives you the impression that she'd rather be somewhere else.

Lana Turner was once a huge Hollywood star but now on the downward slope. Years before, Turner had famously been spotted by a Hollywood reporter sipping Coke in a café after skipping a typing class in school. He was astonished by her beauty and poise and passed her details onto talent agent (and former Marx Brothers star) Zeppo Marx. Turner was soon a Hollywood legend and film star. Lana might seem bored but Ralph Bates is quite good in Persecution as her strange son. Roles like this were comfortably in the wheelhouse of Ralph

Bates. One big problem with this film is that you don't really care much about any of the characters (not even the cat loving Lana) or the mystery concerning the specifics of their strange relationship. The last part of the film is supposed to be quite dramatic as all these revelations are dumped on the viewer but by this stage I was clock watching and desperate for the bell to ring.

I have to confess that I didn't like all the cat stuff in this film. I have cats and I hate watching films where cats are in peril or harmed. They should keep animals out of horror films because if someone puts a cat or dog in peril or harms them in a film then my first inclination is to go to the fast forward button and skip this scene. I know it isn't real but I hate stuff like this. Maim and kill all the humans you want in horror films but leave the animals out of it. My sympathies were definitely with Lana Turner rather than Ralph Bates in this film due to her love of cats. At nearly one hour and forty minutes this film is longer than it really needs to be. This is one of those film where at some point your eyes start to glaze over and you keep checking to see how much more of this you have to endure before the ending looms on the horizon.

Persecution does perk up though when Olga Georges-Picot is introduced as Monique Kalfon. Monique is a sexy French woman who Carrie hires to be a nurse for her son's ill wife. In reality what Carrie has really hired Monique to do is seduce her son and therefore wreck his marriage. David is only human and soon succumbs to the Gallic charms of Monique.

Olga Georges-Picot had her most famous role a year later as the Countess who seduces Woody Allen in Love and Death. Persecution is a lot more fun with Olga Georges-Picot in the film but then sags a bit when she leaves. Carrie meeting Monique is quite amusing because she spies her in some sort of naff restaurant disco (the sort of place that only exists in films). Carrie takes her beloved cat with her - on a lead of course. I'm assuredly no expert on restaurants but I'm pretty sure you wouldn't be allowed in a swanky restaurant with a cat! If I popped down to my nearest restaurant with one of my cats I'm fairly sure I would not be permitted to dine at this establishment seated next to a moggy.

Suzan Farmer, who made a couple of Hammer films, is fine as David's wife and future voiceover king Patrick Allen pops up in the film too. On the whole, I can't say I enjoyed Persecution very much. This is a strange and dull film that becomes something of an endurance test to get through in the end with its lame mystery, unsympathetic characters, and sedate pacing. The thing I dislike most about this film above all else is that the screenwriter is clearly not a big fan of cats! It's hard to say who Persecution is supposed to be aimed at. There isn't much here for horror fans so I'd probably say that Persecution is strictly for Lana Turner completists only.

RAWHEAD REX (1986)

Rawhead Rex was directed by George Pavlou from a screenplay by Clive Barker. It is based on Barker's short story of the same name. Clive Barker disliked this film and felt it was too tame and also badly made. He thought the subtext and visceral horror of his story was absent in the film. I'm with Clive Barker on this one and am not a fan of this film either. Barker's story was set in rural Kent in the summer. The people behind this film made it in Ireland to save money and also shot it in the winter - which would partly explain why everything seems washed out and bleak. Barker complained that the people behind this film locked him out of the creative process and wouldn't let him visit the set. This is certainly odd because if you have famed horror author Clive Barker writing your horror film surely you'd like to have his input wouldn't you? I would but the makers of this film didn't. They just wanted to make the film their own way and for Barker to keep his beak out.

There was a big upside to this though because the frustration of 1985's Underworld and Rawhead Rex motivated Barker to direct Hellraiser and have creative control over an adaptation of one of his stories. Hellraiser is a horror masterpiece so maybe in hindsight we should be grateful to Rawhead Rex for paving the way to Hellraiser. Rawhead Rex is a British film but was made in Ireland with mostly Irish actors. This film is definitely not the most realistic or cliché light depiction of Ireland in 1986. You have comical farmers and drunken bumpkins who live in caravans. One of the Irish police officers seems to have a Sten gun when they respond to an emergency. What is this, 1943? The plot revolves around Howard Hallenbeck (David Dukes). Howard is an American staying in a rural part of Ireland with his family to research an old church for a book he is writing.

Howard's family aren't having much fun but he loves it in Ireland and is fascinated by his religious research. Anyway, it transpires that in the nearby countryside a fearsome creature named Rawhead Rex has been resurrected by lightning. Howard's research at the church might be the key to defeating the creature. This film version of Rawhead Rex seems to have a small cult following but it's hard to see why because it isn't much fun. I described the creature as 'fearsome' just now and that is definitely misleading because Rex in this film is anything but fearsome. It's just a tall stuntman/actor wearing a terrible rubber monster mask. Rex stumbles around so clumsily and so slowly it's hard to imagine how he would ever actually catch anyone. A big chunk of this film is literally just a rubber masked monster lumbering around in the woods.

There isn't even the saving grace of lashings of gore or memorable kills. It could be the case that the makers of Rawhead Rex were treading lightly because of the video nasty hysteria. They needed a film suitable for video release because that was where most of their profit was coming from. You can see this film didn't have much of a budget. The special effects sequence at the end is atrocious even for 1986. I didn't care too much for the performances in this film although Ronan Wilmott as the nutty verger is to be commended for at least trying to inject some life into this affair. The late David Dukes is not a terribly interesting lead but I did enjoy his cardigans and knitwear.

I think the problem with adapting Rawhead Rex is that it is difficult to do a faithful adaptation because in the story the monster is sexual in design and goes around biting the heads off children. The makers of this film steer clear of that (a child is attacked - but offscreen) and are also less interested in the origins of the monster than the original story. Clive Barker has expressed an interest in a new film version - which might work better today because CGI could be used to make the creature more like the book version and you could probably get away with more darkness and violence in a modern version. Some people seem to like the Rawhead Rex film and think it is good for a few laughs and that's fine because we all have our personal likes and dislikes. This film just didn't do it for me though and I found it a fairly tedious experience to be honest. If you like low-budget retro monster films there many out there way better than Rawhead Rex.

RAZOR BLADE SMILE (1998)

Razor Blade Smile was written and directed by Jake West. West later directed, among other things, the forgettable Danny Dyer horror film Doghouse. I like Jake West as a horror documentary filmmaker but I don't like any of the actual horror films he has made. Razor Blade Smile, which looks like it had a budget of about 10 bob, was his debut and is pretty obscure. This is basically a B film. The sort of film that played at a horror festival and then vanished into thin air. It is like watching an elaborate fan film or a cheap short film dragged out into a feature. The plot concerns Lilith Silver (Eileen Daly) - who is a vampire and about 150 years old. Lilith works as a contract killer and her targets are members of the Illuminati who have connections to the family who murdered her lover years ago. Or something like that. She keeps an arsenal of guns in her coffin and wears a PVC catsuit when she goes off to shoot people. To be honest, I'm probably making this film sound a lot more entertaining than it actually is.

Razor Blade Smile looks like a cheap 1980s pop video made and edited by someone having a seizure. The lighting is no existent and the performances in the film are amateurish and wooden. One of the things I dislike about films like this is that they try to disguise their incompetence by being crazy, incoherent and stupid and thus beg us to treat it as a laugh or a cult film. You can't intentionally make a cult film. You just make a film and it is up to future audiences to decide if that film has become a cult film. Razor Blade Smile is not a cult film or a guilty pleasure B film. It is just a bad film. Now, admittedly, you can cut Razor Blade Smile some slack on account of the fact that Jake West plainly had no resources at all at his disposal when he made this film. You can see he's thrown the kitchen sink (though a very small kitchen sink with minuscule leaky taps given his budget) at Razor Blade Smile and tried to make it goofy and over the top. B+ for effort then but D- for execution.

I didn't have the faintest idea who any of the cast in Razor Blade Smile were - well, except for David Warbeck, who pops up here in a smallish part. Sadly, this was the last thing David Warbeck ever did. He was best known for the cult films he made in Italy and also apparently came close to playing James Bond a couple of times. I would say it was sad that this was his last role but knowing him he probably wouldn't have minded bowing out in a daft low-budget horror film. It could have been worse. At least he didn't end up in Doctors or Hollyoaks. Eileen

Daly is the vampish heroine of the film and throws herself into the role but she doesn't have much charisma and her line delivery is as wooden as a telegraph pole. Christopher Adamson, who plays Sethane Blake, was the serial killer Leo Rook in the film 1999 horror film Lighthouse (which we discussed earlier).

The gunplay in the film is very inspired by the Tarantino films of the early 1990s and John Woo. Razor Blade Smile feels a lot like a dusty relic of its era now. It's a film aimed at Loaded readers who liked Reservoir Dogs. There's probably a bit too much plot in Razor Blade Smile given this is an action vampire film and the jokes dispensed by Lillith are no threat to Oscar Wilde. There is gore, blood, gunplay, crazy camera shots. None of it really lands though and some of the practical effects are quite poor. Some people might get a kick out of this film and that's fine but there is something too self-satisfied about Razor Blade Smile for me which made it unlikeable. It thinks it is an outrageous laugh but in reality is a bit boring. The same year that Razor Blade Smile came out saw the release of Stephen Norrington's action vampire film Blade. If you desire to watch someone in leather outfits shoot people in a vampire film here is my advice. Go and watch Blade again and give Razor Blade Smile a wide berth!

Jake West also directed (the television sequel) Pumpkinhead: Ashes to Ashes and Evil Aliens. None of Jake West's films are any good in my opinion. None of them add anything to the British horror film landscape. His work as as an editor on horror documentaries though has been very laudable and educational. I would certainly recommend watching his documentary Video Nasties: Moral Panic, Censorship & Videotape. It was with horror documentaries that Jake West found his calling. Razor Blade Smile feels a lot like a nice title in search of a film or a story. I didn't like this film but maybe you'll get more fun out of it than me. By the way, not long after this film came out we got the (awful) Underworld series with

Kate Beckinsale as a vampire in a catsuit shooting people. I wonder if the makers of Underworld watched Razor Blade Smile?

THE ROAD BUILDER (1971)

The Road Builder (aka The Night Digger) was directed by Alastair Reid. This is a fairly obscure film (in Britain at any rate because because I have no memories of ever watching this on television anywhere) but it is an interesting thriller which deserves more recognition than it ever managed to attain. The film's relative obscurity is somewhat puzzling because it was written by Roald Dahl. Dahl wrote the film for his wife Patricia Neal to star in. At the time she was recovering from a stroke. Roald Dahl wasn't a big fan of how this film turned out and blamed the director Alastair Reid for its failure. Reid, in turn, aimed a few barbs back at Dahl. Despite all of this drama and finger pointing though the film is actually pretty good. This is one of those early seventies British films that for some reason has yet to be rediscovered and given any credit.

In the film Patricia Neal plays Maura Prince, a lonely woman who looks after her elderly blind mother Edith (Pamela Brown). A young man on a motorcycle named Billy (Nicholas Clay) turns up inquiring about working as a handyman. Billy said he had heard about the job from a neighbour. Despite her initial reluctance, Maura gives Billy some work and he turns out to be a good grafter and a decent young man. Edith takes a shine to him too and assumes Billy must be a relative. However, Billy is hiding a dark secret. He is actually a serial killer and tormented by demons in his past. The question becomes a case of how much Maura suspects Billy and how much she might be willing to let slide merely to keep his company around.

The Road Builder is a very watchable film which goes down

some dark alleyways. It has that raw early seventies quality although there is nice some location work in Cornwall too.

This is probably the best part that Nicholas Clay ever had. He later became best known for playing Lancelot in John Boorman's Excalibur and was also in Evil Under the Sun (a film I inevitably end up watching each Christmas when it is wheeled out on telly yet again). I always remember Clay most for his role in the Child's Play episode of Hammer House of Mystery & Suspense. This is the bonkers episode where a family wake up and find themselves trapped in their house by an impenetrable wall. In his roles, Clay was usually posh and handsome and somewhat wooden. Though he was interviewed for the part of James Bond in the early 1980s he never became a big star. Anyway, in The Road Builder we see a different side of Clay. He isn't posh or suave. He's an everyman - well except for the serial killer stuff.

Patricia Neal and Pamela Brown are both good in the film too. Despite the fact Edith is supposed to be the elderly mother and Maura the daughter, Brown was only about eight years older than Neal in real life. There are, as you tend to expect of old British films, a number of familiar faces in the supporting parts. Yootha Joyce is Mrs Palafox. Yootha was already a prolific actor in many things. The Road Builder was two years shy of Yootha Joyce taking the part of Mildred Roper in Man About the House - which led to George & Mildred. Brigit Forsyth also pops up as a nurse. This would have been a few years before she became a familiar face for her role as Thelma in Whatever Happened to the Likely Lads? As if that wasn't enough you also get Peter Sallis as Reverend Rupert Palafox. This was two years before he took the part of Cleggy in Last of the Summer Wine. It's a bit of a strange coincidence that The Road Builder contains all these actors who were about to become nationally famous thanks to sitcoms.

The Road Builder is an absorbing drama/thriller and although not a pure horror film it does have horror film elements. The one disappointing thing about the film is that the ending feels slightly underwhelming. Given that this film was written by Roald Dahl you unavoidably find yourself expecting some dark kicker of a twist at the end which whips the rug out from under your feet. The really odd thing about The Road Builder is that no one involved in the film seemed to have a good word to say about it. Patricia Neal hated the film and, as we mentioned, Roald Dahl and Alastair Reid did not look back on it with fond memories. The Road Builder is a good film though if you ask me and worth watching if you've never encountered it before. I can't help wondering if this film's obscurity has something to do with it having such an underwhelming title. If they'd called it Night Killer or something it would probably be much better known and more cultish.

SCHIZO (1976)

Schizo was directed by Pete Walker and written by David McGillivray. You wouldn't call the Pete Walker films 'forgotten' these days as they are very well known and cultish today in horror fan circles but they were never mainstream and never got as much love as they deserved at the time. Schizo is arguably one of the somewhat lesser discussed of Walker's films - at least compared to Frightmare and House of Whipcord. The story in Schizo revolves around a famous ice skater named Samantha Gray (Lynne Frederick) who is about to be married to a carpet warehouse businessman named Alan Falconer (John Leyton). Alan has a nice blazer at work but at home favours navy blue denim outfits which are more 1970s than a packet of Spangles and some Angel Delight.

Apart from a brief scene at the start we don't see Samantha ice skating or training. It is basically just a device to make Samantha famous and someone whose marriage might be reported in a newspaper - which is how a certain William

Haskin (Jack Watson) learns of this news. Haskin is a morose and depressed man who seems to be working as a docker in Newcastle. He lives in a grubby flat which looks like something out of 1894. Haskin is clearly angered when he reads of Samantha's marriage. He decides to take a train to London - packing a big cleaver and a broken glass in his suitcase. But what is he planning to do and what is his connection to the young ice skater?

We should probably say straight off the bat that Schizo does not present the most realistic or factual depiction of schizophrenia. This is a Pete Walker horror film so not to be taken too seriously. Schizo is a slasher film (and two years before Halloween to boot) with Italian influences blended into the typically English milieu of Pete Walker's horror world. What makes this slightly different from Walker's previous films is that he goes for more of a Hitchcock suspense murder mystery here with red herrings abounding all over the shop. You still (happily) get murder, gore, and lots of blood and nastiness though. If you like Pete Walker's films then Schizo is very enjoyable on the whole but it does have a couple of problems. One problem is the length. This film is ten minutes shy of two hours and didn't really need to be that long.

The other problem is that the identity of the killer in the film is not exactly difficult to work out. The title rather gives it away too one might argue. I deduced very quickly the real situation regarding Haskin and Samantha and the film never whipped the rug out from under me - though it does set up multiple possible suspects. Schizo has a great cast to play this material. Lynne Frederick, who had a tragic end and became a pariah in the film industry and beyond after marrying Peter Sellers and not giving any of his money to his children when he died (she was basically seen, whether fairly or unfairly, as a shameless and selfish young gold-digger), is captured here at a point in her career when she seemed destined for stardom. She is beautiful and has a likeable understated acting style in this film. I enjoyed too Samantha's range of 1970s leather jackets and flares. Apparently, Lynne Frederick just wore her own clothes in the film to save the production money.

John Fraser is terrific as the psychiatrist Leonard and good old Stephanie Beacham plays a friend of Samantha and Alan. Queenie Watts steals every scene she is in as Samantha's cockney cleaner and Jack Watson manages to navigate the tricky task of playing a part in which he hardly has any dialogue until the end. Watson is good at the end when he finally (finally!) has some dialogue. One scene which doesn't work though is a flashback where Haskin is supposed to be much younger. They put a rather silly wig on Watson and pretend he's twenty years younger. John McEnery, who has a cameo as a nutty patient of Leonard, was married to Stephanie Beacham when this film came out - which probably explains the cameo. This nutty patient is yet another red herring in the film. There are so many red herrings in the film that you do second guess your initial deductions.

Schizo is unusual for a Pete Walker film in that there is a supernatural horror scene when Queenie's clairvoyant daughter Joy (Trisha Mortimer) channels a killer at a spiritualist group meeting. Her eyes turn silver and huge, the wind picks up - smashing a door in - and her voice turns strange. It's a great sequence and unexpected too given that this is a Walker film. There is plenty of nudity in the film (the camera lingers on Samantha taking a shower at one point) and some memorable deaths. The film's greatest kill is surely the death by knitting needle - a wonderfully implausible and nasty showstopper. A woman is bludgeoned with a hammer at a bus stop (and then thrown under a bus!), a man has his throat slashed while sat in his car at traffic lights, there is a gruesome blood drenched stabbing in a flashback scene. Suffice to say, Schizo doesn't disappoint when it comes to gore and violence.

Schizo is great fun with the London locations and 1970s

atmosphere (I love Samantha's white telly - in a big wooden box with doors). It's just a shame it wasn't a bit shorter. There are, for me, a few too many scenes where Samantha is menaced or spooked by something and then when help arrives they find that nothing is there. They do this three or four times in the film and it gets a bit tiresome in the end. Still, the scene in the supermarket (a Wallis supermarket in case any supermarket spotters are curious) where Samantha is spooked by someone calling her name is well done. Schizo is not perfect but it is very enjoyable on the whole. This is a very watchable and blood drenched British slasher film made at a time when the slasher boom had yet to kick in. You could say then that Schizo was somewhat ahead of its time.

SCREAM FOR HELP (1984)

Scream for Help is a thriller film written by Tom Holland (who wrote Psycho II and wrote and directed 1985's Fright Night). It would probably be pushing it to call Scream for Help a horror film although it is usually billed as such. Although the film is set in the United States with an American cast it was actually a British film and mostly made in Berkshire. There was some location shooting though in New Rochelle, New York - specifically for the car sequence. I was drawn to this film because of the Tom Holland link and its billing as a British horror film. A major problem though is that it was directed by Michael Winner. If you had to handpick someone to expertly adapt a suspenseful Tom Holland script it probably wouldn't be Michael Winner would it?

My research indicates that Michael Winner was full of his customary chutzpah promoting Scream for Help and said it was as scary as Friday the 13th. It isn't though. It really isn't. Scream for Help concerns a teenager named Christie Cromwell (Rachael Kelly) who lives with her mother Karen (Marie Masters) in a very plush house. Life should be good for

Christie but she isn't happy at all. The main problem is her stepfather Paul (David Allen Brooks). Christie is convinced that Paul, despite pretending to be nice, is actually a fraud and a conman and is plotting to murder her mother for a financial windfall. But will anyone believe her?

The plot of Scream for Help is not exactly original. This is classic television thriller film fodder - which is slightly odd as you'd expect something a bit more clever from Tom Holland. Maybe something was lost in translation and with a better director this could have been much better. Much of the film is taken up with Christie following Paul around and trying to get evidence that he's having an affair and doesn't really love her mother. This part of the film is passable entertainment but it isn't exactly Rear Window in the suspense stakes. It helps that Rachael Kelly (who didn't have any acting credits after this film) is likeable as Christie and David Allen Brooks is also quite good as the cheesy and insincere Paul. There ias a lot of narration by Christie in the film because we hear her diary entries.

What doesn't help is the jaunty music score - which feels like it belongs in a comedy film or on Love Boat or something rather than a thriller. Christie enlists the help of her friend Janey (Sandra Clark) and Janey's boyfriend Josh (Corey Parker). Although he's supposed to nice, Josh, like many male teenagers in 1980s films, comes off a bit creepy and date rapey to say the least. Talk about a one track mind. All the air goes out of Scream for Help when Paul is revealed to be a maniac fraud. The last act of the film is an interminable hostage caper (Michael Winner always did love a good home invasion) with Christie and her wheelchair bound mother (she broke her foot falling down the stairs) trapped in their home by Paul, Brenda (the woman Paul is having an affair with and played by Lolita Lorre - that can't be her real name surely?), and Brenda's husband Lacey (Rocco Sisto) - who Paul thinks is Brenda's brother. Are you keeping up with any of this? There is friction between this dodgy trio - which Christie tries to turn to her advantage.

There is an unintentionally funny moment in Scream for Help when Paul pushes Christie's mother down the basement stairs and she tumbles out of her wheelchair like a Benny Hill sketch. A scene earlier in the film where Karen falls down the stairs is also amusing because you can plainly see it is really a stuntman wearing a wig and a dress. About two thirds of the way into Scream for Help I was bored and ready for the film to end. The script is designed to have these twists and tense situations but it is executed in a way that simply makes it boring. It is possible I suppose that with a better director, a better (and more appropriate) music score, and a better cast (the actors playing Paul and Brenda are not very good) that Scream for Help could have been a decent little film. There is a sprinkling of sex and nudity in the film but not much. Michael Winner, by his own pervy standards, is quite restrained.

As far as violence goes in Scream for Help there are a few stabbings but not much blood. The biggest shock moment in the film comes when a character is hit by a car and tumbles to the floor covered in blood. The whole film is essentially building up to the constrictive captive drama at the end but this somehow turns out to be the most tedious part of the film. I enjoyed the early scenes of Christie playing detective far more than I did the last act. Scream for Help is not an especially memorable film and there is probably no good reason to go out of your way to watch it. As far as the Michael Winner back catalogue goes,

I'd much rather watch Death Wish 3 again that sit through A Scream for Help a second time. At least Death Wish 3 is stupidly entertaining and has Charles Bronson blowing people up with a rocket launcher.

SCREAMTIME (1983)

This is a curious horror anthology with a slightly mysterious existence. Three short British films by Michael Armstrong and Stanley A Long are turned into a compendium with a bizarre new framing sequence in New York that someone cobbled together as a wraparound. Three New Yorkers (one is a beer guzzling oaf and another is a buxom lady who we gratuitously see taking a shower at the start) steal three horror videos and these turn out to be the films we see in the segments. It's not much of a wraparound but you have to give someone credit for coming up with the idea of lacing these short films together.

In the first story - That's the Way to Do It - Robin Bailey is a veteran Punch & Judy man named Jack who doesn't get much respect from his family. His puppet capers are not paying the bills and his wife wants to move to Canada. His stepson Damien (how appropriate) is a spiteful punk and played by Jonathon Morris, an actor British viewers might know for the 80s Liverpudlian sitcom Bread. Damien decides to burn down Jack's puppet stand and do away with his puppets. This leads to a puppet revenge rampage of murder. Has Mr Punch come to life or has Jack gone crackers? This is as daft as it sounds but if you can't glean some entertainment from a cricket bat wielding puppet then there is probably no hope for you. This segment has a really downbeat sort of aura and some seaside location work.

Next we have a haunted house mystery titled Dreamhouse with young couple Tony (Ian Saynor) and Susan (Yvonne Nicholson) Kingsley moving into a new home and quickly realising something is wrong. Blood abounds, a spooky child rides a bike around, a man with a knife is glimpsed rushing past the bedroom. I'd definitely ask for a discount on the rent. This story is impressively eerie and has a twist that is worth waiting for. It's a pretty solid haunted house mystery. You could imagine this as an episode of Hammer House of Horror if it was made in a slightly tamer way. Dreamhouse is definitely the bloodiest of the segments on offer in Screamtime and has a few moments worthy of a 'video nasty'.

Finally, we have Do You Believe in Fairies? - the tale of a bike racer who desperately needs money and decides to rob kind old Mildred (Jean Anderson) and Emma (Dora Bryan) after they give him a job as a handyman. However, these dotty old ladies seem to believe in fairies, ghosts and, um, killer garden gnomes. This is predictable but quite good fun. The bike racing villain is played by David Van Day, a rather naff pop star of the era. Some pretty good zombie type effects in this segment. There's a rather surreal and weird interlude near the end featuring a love scene but - generally - this is a watchable tale of karmic just desserts in the anthology tradition. We then go back to the trio in New York and, well, you'll just have to see what happens to them for yourself. Screamtime is a strange film it has to be said. A bit grubby and homemade but genuinely creepy at times. It's worth a look for the anthology completist.

THE SENDER (1982)

The Sender was directed by Roger Christian and written by Thomas Baum. This film sank without trace in 1982 but seems to have something of a cult following these days. The director Roger Christian was a second unit director on a couple of Star Wars films and later had to suffer the indignity of being the man who directed the infamous Battlefield Earth. If you watched The Sender and Battlefield Earth one after the other with no knowledge of either you'd have no idea they were directed by the same person. The Sender is an unusual and well made psychological horror thriller while Battlefield Earth is, well, Battlefield Earth. The Sender is a difficult film to describe. It is sort of like

One Flew Over the Cuckoo's Nest crossed with A Nightmare On Elm Street - which is impressive given that Nightmare on Elm was still two years away at the time. Parts of this film vaguely reminded me of The Dead Zone too.

The film begins with a young man (Željko Ivanek) attempting to drown himself in a lake. He is taken to a mental institution but is suffering from amnesia and has no idea who he is. The hospital therefore refer to him as John Doe #83. The psychiatrist Dr Gail Farmer (Kathryn Harrold) takes an interest in the young man because it soon becomes apparent there is something very strange about him. He can 'send' his nightmares and dreams into the heads of other people - which make them experience vivid hallucinations. Gail and

John Doe #83 both have visions of his mother Jerolyn (Shirley Knight). This woman clearly holds the key to discovering what exactly happened to this most unusual patient...

The Sender is quite a slow burn sort of film and probably won't be everyone's cup of tea. Though there are horror elements it is more of a weird supernatural mystery film than anything and the story is built around us (slowly) discovering what happened between John Doe #83 and his mother. What helps a lot is that the film has a great cast. Željko Ivanek and Kathryn Harrold are both very good and solid support is on hand with Paul Freeman as Dr Joseph Denman. This must have been the first thing Freeman did after Raiders of the Lost Ark. By the way, look out for Al Matthews as Herb. Al Matthews was later Sergeant Apone in Aliens. There have been a lot of horror films (and films in general) set in mental institutions but The Sender is unique enough to have its own identity and stand out from many of them. The hallucinations triggered by John Doe #83 make for some striking and highly alarming moments in the film.

The memorable highlight of The Sender comes when Dr

Denman decides to use shock therapy on John Doe #83 and all hell breaks loose when the electrodes are attached. Glass shatters and all the doctors begin flying through the air in slow motion. This is a remarkable and strange sequence shot with great flair. This institution never quite seems to learn any lessons because when they try surgery on John Doe #83 later on the whole operating theatre bursts into flames. You'd probably describe this film as unsettling rather than downright scary but it has plenty of atmosphere and the institution is spooky while still being vaguely realistic. Some of the surgery scenes are quite unpleasant and there is a hallucination decapitation (by punch) though the practical effect for this scene could have been better. You can see why A Nightmare On Elm Street is sometimes speculated to have been influenced by The Sender to some degree because both films have the premise of people becoming immersed in horrific situations through hallucinations and dreams.

The Sender has plenty of scenes set outside the institution - which helps open the film up and make it feel like a bigger story. There's a car chase and the opening scene where John Doe #83 tries to drown himself in a lake as bemused tourists look on is quite effective. The Sender is quite an absorbing film and full of memorable moments. I'm not sure if you would quite say this is some lost masterpiece but it is one of those films that didn't deserve to be so ignored and obscure. Roger Christian had to fight to stop the studio editing the film in a radically different way and he was unhappy at the lack of promotion. It wouldn't surprise me if the studio had no idea how to market The Sender because it isn't your run of the mill horror film. This is an interesting and at times arresting and stylish film with a very good cast. It is certainly worth a look. I should point out though that while The Sender is a British film it doesn't feel much like one with the American setting and characters.

THE SHE BEAST (1966)

The She Beast was the directorial debut of Michael Reeves - who would go on to make The Sorcerers and Witchfinder General before sadly dying far too young. The She Beast was made in about 20 days on a tiny budget and I'd be lying if I said that wasn't apparent when watching this amateurish film. The basic plot has an English couple named Philip (Ian Ogilvy) and Veronica (Barbara Steele) on their honeymoon in Transylvania. After a car accident, Veronica is taken over by the vengeful spirit of Vardella - a witch who was executed 200 years ago. If he is to have any chance of getting Veronica back, Philip will have to learn to trust a certain Count Von Helsing (John Karlsen)...

The She Beast was such a cheapjack production that Michael Reeves had to use his own money to get it finished. Barbara Steele was only hired for one day so what did was keep her on the production for eighteen straight hours so they could shoot as many scenes with her character as possible. This apparently annoyed her no end. The She Beast is one of those films where everyone sounds dubbed and half the time you have no idea what is going on. The editing is bizarre and there is a car chase sequence which is speeded up and looks like something out of a comedy show. I gather that Michael Reeves was mortified when he viewed this car chase sequence but he didn't have the money to do it over so just had to keep it in the film.

One of the problems with this film (and there are many) is that you can't quite work out what Reeves is actually going for. The start of the film is your classic Gothic old time horror but then when we cut to the modern day with have a number of comedy scenes with the bumbling police officers and locals in Transylvania. This makes the film all over the place in terms of its tone and none of the comedy is funny. Given that this film takes place in what was still a Soviet satellite state at the time one can possibly read a criticism of the communist system (or at least the Soviet communist system) in the depiction of the bungling and drunken locals.

The film relies a lot on John Karlsen as Van Helsing because not only does he have to deliver all the exposition he seems to be the only actor in the film who is trying to give a professional performance and take any of this seriously. Ian Ogilvy does not appear to be taking the film that seriously and delivers a very wooden performance. You can probably cut Ian Ogilvy some slack because this was the start of his acting career and he did this film as a favour to his friend Michael Reeves. I'm not sure Ogilvy even knows what The She Beast is supposed to be and for that he can't really be blamed.

Having talked about how cheap and incoherent this film is do I have anything good to say about it? Well, the mask used for Vardella is creepy and the opening of the film is quite effective in a melodramatic and low-budget sort of way. This film might have worked better as a period piece about witchcraft - although whether Reeves had the money and resources to do that is open to question. If you are drawn to this film because of Barbara Steele you might be disappointed she isn't in the film for longer. Because they only hired her for one day and her character is replaced by a vengeful witch she unavoidably disappears for a good chunk of the running time. The She Beast is a very grainy looking film with some of the indoors scenes very dark and crackly (though thankfully much of it takes place outdoors).

The She Beast is a very short film and runs to around 80 minutes (depending on which version you watch). This indicates that Michael Reeves barely had sufficient footage for a feature length film and provides an explanation for why he left the daft car chase in. The She Beast is quite a dull and perplexing film on the whole and becomes a slog to get through long before the running time is over. If you like strange zero budget films you might get more out this than me though so have a look for yourself if you've never sampled the curious and oddball oddity that is The She Beast.

THE SHOUT (1978)

The Shout was directed by Jerzy Skolimowski and based on a short story by Robert Graves. The film begins with a nice game of cricket. It turns out though that this game is being played at some sort of mental institution (or loony bin as one of the schoolgirls from Killer's Moon would have it) and is a game between patients and staff. A member of staff name Graves (played by a very young looking Tim Curry) is in the scorer's shed and ends up chatting to a mysterious man named Crossley (Alan Bates). Crossley claims that an Aboriginal shaman taught him how to perform a 'shout' so powerful it would be deadly. The film revolves around Crossley's tale of how he invaded the life of a composer named

Anthony Fielding (John Hurt) and basically took over his home - which Anthony shared with his wife Rachel (Susannah York).

Crossley says he tells variations on this story but they are all the same. Is he a reliable narrator or this all just a figment of his imagination? And who is Crossley anyway? Is he a patient? Don't expect answers to the many questions posed by The Shout. It is really up to the viewer to decide for themselves if Crossley is possessed of dark magic or merely a creative fantasist. The bulk of the film has Crossley worming his way into the home of Fielding and then gradually taking over - even stealing his wife. The way Crossley tells this story it was all done through magic but we question whether it happened at all.

The Shout is a very strange film and fairly obscure (I can't recall ever watching this on television) but it does seem to have a modest cult following. The story takes place in ruggedly beautiful locations in North Devon and there is an amazing cast. The cricket match also features Robert Stephens as the medical officer and a young Jim Broadbent as one of the fielders. A lightning strike at the end of the match might be a natural event or it might have been Crossley's magic. It's all ambiguous. Fielding is a composer of electronic music and the scenes of him doing this are fascinating and weird. The Shout did this sort of thing long before Berberian Sound Studio. Tony Banks and Mike Rutherford from Genesis did the score for the film and the sound design is very atmospheric.

John Hurt and Susannah York are good in the film but this is really the Alan Bates show and he's suitably enigmatic, charismatic, and strange as the sinister Crossley. Fielding becomes interested in Crossley because of his tales of being able to produce a unique sound (a shout) but he comes to regret being a soft touch and inviting Crossley for lunch when the stranger never leaves and begins to displace him from his own home. Fielding must find a way to combat the unfathomable threat posed by Crossley but how one would go about that is not easy to say. The sequence where Crossley finally dispenses his fabled 'shout' on some lonely sand dunes is a memorable and striking moment which is worth the wait. This film will not be everyone's cup of tea and is more of a psychological drama than a conventional horror film but it is strangely compelling and beautifully made.

The Shout is not an especially long film but it does get under your skin and linger in the memory in a way that few films do. It is just a very bizarre and unusual film and so a fascinating experience if you've never seen it before. Despite its relative lack of fame, The Shout is generally quite well regarded and won a few awards when it came out. It was never the sort of thing that that was likely to make much money or get a huge following - which probably explains why it never became especially famous. The Shout is very well known these days though in cult horror film circles and seems to be getting the attention it deserved but was largely denied back in 1978.

SLEEPWALKER (1984)

Sleepwalker is a fifty minute film directed by Saxton Lagan. Logan went off to make documentaries after this - which is a shame. No one knew what to make of Sleepwalker when it came out and the same is true today. This film was very obscure until fairly recently. Siblings named Marion (Heather Page) and Alex (Bill Douglas) live in a rustic house named Albion which seems to be falling apart. You can detect a few political themes already can't you? A couple named Angela (Joanna David) and Richard (Nickolas Grace) arrive at the house for dinner. Richard is like that Harry Enfield character loadsamoney and a Tory capitalist right down to his braces. Alex on the other hand is an armchair socialist. Friction between this pair is therefore inevitable.

After dinner is ruined by a window falling on their dinner (I hate it when that happens!), the four go out to eat and end up in eatery where Fulton Mckay is the boss. Richard launches into a rant at Alex and Marion joins in too. Later on, there is a bloodbath in the house but is any of this real? Sleepwalker defies any sort of description and is rather baffling. Most people tend to describe this as Mike Leigh meets Dario Argento. That's a very high compliment if you ask me. To merge different styles and yet still make something that feels cohesive and connective is not easy.

The performances in the film are deliberately exaggerated and the turn into horror at the end something makes the whole thing a memorably weird and unfathomable sort of experience - which was probably the point. Nickolas Grace, who plays Richard in the film, was a familiar face in the 1980s as he played the Sheriff of Nottingham in Robin of Sherwood. The title of this film comes from the fact that Alex sleepwalks. Sleepwalker is engaging and watchable even before the horror antics kick in. The director is clearly not a fan of Margaret Thatcher and this film was made at a time when she seemed set to be in charge forever after the Falklands War turned her fortunes around. On the evidence of this film Saxton Logan was a very talented and interesting filmmaker. Sadly though his career (in films) never took off. It would have been interesting to have seen him make a full length horror film.

SYMPTOMS (1974)

Symptoms was written and directed by directed by José Ramón Larraz. There was a period when this was considered a lost film but thankfully it is quite easy to find these days. Symptoms is still quite unknown though which is a shame because you could argue that this is one of the best British horror films ever made. The story takes place in a somewhat ramshackle country mansion which belongs to the family estate of a young woman named Helen Ramsey (Angela Pleasence). We learn Helen hasn't been very well recently and it is implied that her illness was mental rather than physical. Helen has invited her friend Anne (Lorna Heilbron) to stay at the house with her for a short while. Anne is a translator and welcomes the chance to have some peace and quiet to do some work.

Anne inquires about a photograph in the house, which Helen tells her is a picture of her friend Cora. Cora isn't around anymore apparently. Despite the tranquil surroundings, Anne begins to hear strange noises in the house and notice that Helen sometimes exhibits odd behaviour. Anne also becomes aware that a handyman named Brady (Peter Vaughan) always seems to be lurking around outside. Brady lives in the stables of the house and seems strangely interested in the activities of Helen. Helen, for some reason, despises Brady and tells Anne that she never speaks to him. What dark secrets lurk in this seemingly idyllic place?

Symptoms is a beautiful looking film with lovely photography. The house echoes the mental fragility of Helen with its dilapidated and isolated aura. The house is also overgrown with vegetation and seems to blending in into its surroundings. The film has an autumnal feel which makes it look very cosy (though there is nothing cosy about the film in the end) and I love the scene where Helen and Anne relax after dinner by a log fire. Sometimes you watch a film where you sort of envy the characters for where they are. Helen's house, a cosy peaceful place with log fires and rambles in the woods, sounds like heaven to me. It obviously doesn't turn out to be heaven though in Symptoms because it wouldn't be much of a horror film if it consisted entirely of two woman relaxing by a log fire.

Symptoms is what you might describe as an arty horror film. The early scenes look more like something out of an Ingmar Bergman film than a 1970s British horror film. Symptoms was supposed to star the doomed icon Jean Seberg *, which would have been interesting, but she was replaced at the last minute by Angela Pleasence. This was a fortuitous turn of events because Angela Pleasence was clearly born to play the part of Helen. There is a strange otherworldly quality to Angela Pleasence which makes her perfect for this film. Helen is fragile and unfathomable. We hardly know anything about her at the start of the film and it becomes a puzzle box for the viewer to get a grip on this character.

Lorna Heilbron, who later married Nicholas Clay in real life, is equally good as Anne. Helen and Anne are two friends who drifted apart but are reconnecting and Pleasence and Heilbron sell that convincingly. Although they seem to get on well it is very apparent that these are two very different people. Anne is charmed by Helen at first but soon begins to pick up on the fact that Helen is still troubled. There is a suggestion of an attraction between the two friends - definitely from Helen. The great Peter Vaughan more than makes the most of his supporting role as Brady and Nancy Nevinson is also good as the housekeeper Hannah. I like Raymond Huntley as Burke too. Burke is the manager of the chemist shop that Helen visits.

Burke and Hannah like to have a bit of a gossip together. Burke's assistant is played by a young Mike Grady - or Barry from Last of the Summer Wine as he's better known.

Symptoms is one of those films that isn't going to be everyone's cup of tea. This is a slow burn mystery that isn't in a rush to go anywhere. I've read reviews of this film where people complain that nothing happens but I don't understand that at all because a LOT happens in the second half of this film. The tone shifts from glacial psychosis drama into more of a full blown horror film. The film Symptoms is often compared to is Repulsion. Symptoms is a difficult film to describe. It's sort of Smiles of a Summer Night blended with Pyscho. The isolation of the location is key to the atmosphere and tone of the film.

There are some very violent scenes in Symptoms in the back half of the film and the attic sequence is wonderfully creepy. Although there is nothing amazingly original about this film it rises about its premise with the great cast, acting, and photography. José Ramón Larraz was for known for making some (often enjoyably) lurid and blood drenched films and Symptoms is fairly restrained by his standards. You could make a strong case for this film being the masterpiece of his career. Symptoms is not for everyone but if you do fall for the languid and mysterious spell the film casts then there are very rich rewards to be found here.

* Jean Seberg became famous in 1956 when Otto Preminger chose her out of 18,000 hopefuls to play Joan of Arc in the 1956 film Saint Joan. Seberg, who was from Iowa, was only seventeen. Although her performance in Saint Joan was unfairly panned she had the last laugh on her critics by becoming a stylish icon through her role in Jean-Luc Godard's Breathless. Her other film roles included Paint Your Wagon and The Mouse That Roared. Seberg's political views, which included public support for the Black Panthers, drew the attention of the FBI and their treatment of her was scandalous.

They put Seberg under surveillance (which made her paranoid) and spread a fake newspaper rumour that father of her impending baby was not her French husband but a Black Panther leader. The FBI memo read - 'The possible publication of Seberg's plight could cause her embarrassment and serve to cheapen her image with the general public'. Seberg suffered a miscarriage and her mental health declined. She killed herself in 1979 in Paris.

TALES THAT WITNESS MADNESS (1972)

Tales That Witness Madness is a British portmanteau horror film from 1973 directed by Freddie Francis. For a long time I thought this film was a strange figment of my imagination but it does exist and has been given a DVD release. This is in the vein of the much better known British anthology horror films (Tales From the Crypt, Vault of Horror, From Beyond the Grave etc) Milton Subotsky produced around the same time for Amicus. With its compendium structure and the presence of Tales From the Crypt director Freddie Francis, Tales That Witness Madness is sometimes mistaken for an Amicus film but actually had nothing at all to do with that cult studio.

This is a reasonable attempt to mimic the Amicus formula and you get a smattering of familiar faces too. Joan Collins, Kim Novak, Frank Forsyth, Donald Pleasance. It does though lack that tongue-in-cheek campy early seventies Amicus sheen (disappointingly, yellow wallpaper and ludicrous neckscarves are thin on the ground here) and the satisfying EC Comics twist in the tale (nasty person gets their comeuppance) is largely absent. The framing device is rather vague and truncated too and not half as much fun as the Amicus ones. Remember Peter Cushing as the eccentric owner of the little antiques shop Temptations Ltd in From Beyond the Grave? Patrick Magee and Robert Powell playing a game of wits in Asylum? The wraparound here is much more forgettable and half-hearted. Still, Tales That Witness Madness is absolutely bonkers at times and worth watching for the infamous third segment alone.

The film begins with a Dr Nicholas (played by Jack Hawkins in his last ever role before he died and he's dubbed by Charles Gray) arriving at the sort of anachronistic and frequently rain lashed maximum security sanatorium for the insane that only seems to exist in seventies British horror films. Dr Nicholas is here to visit his colleague Dr Tremayne (Donald Pleasance) as Tremayne claims to have made some sort of breakthrough treating the assorted lunatics, I mean patients, who have been confined to the institution. He introduces Nicholas to four patients who he believes are vital for his research.

Why are they vital and what exactly does his research involve? I have no idea to be honest because they never really explain. He could be testing their tolerance for Pot Noodles for all I know. We see Hawkins react to each patient's story ("This is the most preposterous thing I have ever heard!") and the Pleasance character seems to suggest this framing device is going somewhere but it never really does save for a predictable coda. Anyway, in the anthology tradition, we get four short horror tales that show us exactly how these patients apparently ended up behind glass in Tremayne's white glazed hospital for the completely insane...

The first story is rather bizarre and called Mr Tiger. The setting is an ordinary suburban house where a boy named Paul (Russell Lewis) retreats ever further (or so it appears on the face of it) into his own fantasy world to shut out the constant and endless bickering, shouting, door slamming and arguing that goes back and forth between his parents (played by Donald Houston and Georgia Brown). Paul now has an imaginary friend that - like all imaginary friends - only he can see.

Nothing wrong with that really. It's some sort of coping mechanism perhaps in a house with a bad tempered workaholic father and boozy mother. But Paul's imaginary friend is a Tiger and he's soon taken to sleeping with the bedroom window open so "Mr Tiger" can come and go as he pleases.

Not only that but he's also leaving giant bones and hunks of meat around the house for his furry invisible chum. The self-absorbed parents don't have too much time for this imaginary friend nonsense but where did those claw marks on the wall come from? Was it Paul or Mr Tiger? Mr Tiger is predictable in the end but I honestly think this would have scared the living daylights out of me if I'd watched it growing up. It feels like a strange kitchen sink drama about domestic neglect/abuse at first but becomes more and more creepy and off-kilter as it progresses. "If Mr Tiger wants to come in here, he'll use the front door like everyone else," says mum, closing Paul's bedroom window for the umpteenth time. Cue a shot of the front door slowly beginning to open on its own! I like the increasingly eerie atmosphere in this segment and while you know exactly where this is going I think Mr Tiger is rather scary despite a few risible props. That little plinky plonky toy piano the child has is very creepy too.

The second story is called Penny Farthing. This is the best looking and most polished of the segments with a good Victorian atmosphere although I have to admit that I couldn't really make head nor tail of the story. A young antiques dealer named Timothy (Peter McEnery) runs a little shop and is left some stuff by a late aunt. A penny farthing bicycle and a photograph of his Uncle Albert (Frank Forsyth), a stern looking Victorian gentleman. Timothy finds that the photograph has a strange power that makes him furiously pedal away on the penny farthing and this keeps transporting him to a Victorian park from the past where he interacts with a widow. It's the old time loop caper but Timothy's unplanned adventures through the past could have alarming consequences for his present.

The story in this segment is somewhat confusing and doesn't appear to have been thought through very much. You could be forgiven for thinking they made this one up on the hoof. It's not bad though and with more of a twist in the tale could easily fit into one of the Amicus compendiums. The penny farthing and antiques shop make for an appropriately anachronistic British atmosphere and they get a lot of mileage out of the portrait of Uncle Albert constantly changing to express different moods. He's a malevolent presence even through the photograph and I expect he might just turn up in that park too. Nothing here makes an awful lot of sense but Peter McEnery (father of Brookside and Ballykissangel actress Kate McEnery) is very good as the young central protagonist and I'm surprised I haven't seen him in more things. Despite the muddled story I found Penny Farthing to be relatively compelling and watchable although I'm not sure this story would be one you could return to much in the way you can watch the Amicus anthologies over and over again. You do get Frank Forsyth as a zombie though and that alone is almost worth the price of admission.

That's two down which means I can finally move onto the third segment Mel - truly the most bizarre and demented story I have ever encountered in one of these anthology films. "Does anyone here love me?" asks Brian (Michael Jayston) at the start of this weird bauble, arriving home after his morning jog. The mutton chopped Beatle fringed Brian lives in an open plan arty country house (albeit on the edge of a very spooky fog shrouded woods) and is married to the Bella (Joan Collins). Life is pretty good for Brian you'd imagine. However, this particular morning he has returned home with a huge tree stump that he decides to plonk in the living room as a strange piece of modern art. The tree trunk looks like it has arms and legs and Brian is soon besotted with "Mel" (as Bella calls it after spying some graffiti on its trunk) - much to the befuddlement of his wife. This marriage obviously isn't big enough for Brian, Bella and a, er, tree trunk, so Bella is soon plotting to do away with this lump of wood that her husband seems to have developed an unlikely erotic obsession with. Hmmn. Words cannot describe how mad this segment is and consequently Mel is by far the most memorable and entertaining of the stories here.

I presume the tree is supposed to be haunted as it does seem to have a life of its own and the battle of wills between said tree and the pouty sulking jealous Joan Collins leads to some enjoyably bonkers sequences (fans of Sam Raimi's Evil Dead will find this segment very interesting I suspect for one particular scene which seems to anticipate the most notorious moment in that 1982 picture). Great bit where Joan Collins is in bed in her ribboned underwear waiting for Jayston but he prefers to be with the tree! The tree is pretty creepy to be honest although it does look like it's an elaborate suit with a person in there and a bit hokey at times. This segment is the only one here that really seems to understand the spirit of seventies British anthology films and its greatest strength is that it doesn't shy away from its ridiculous premise. It also has a great punchline of an ending. Sure, you'll probably spot the twist coming but it doesn't detract from the fun. I give Mel 27 stars out of a possible 10.

The last segment is called Luau and is by far my least favourite of the four stories. We have a tropical backdrop for this one, the story revolving around a literary agent named Auriol and played by Vertigo star Kim Novak. Novak apparently came out of retirement for this film. A cheapo British horror (that no one remembers today) seems like a fairly bizarre choice of comeback but I digress. Auriol is throwing a big party and banquet for her new client, an oleaginous rake named Kimo (Michael Petrovich) who has an ever present assistant in the form of Keoki (Leon Lissek). Auriol is determined to make a good impression on Kimo but it soon becomes apparent that he's far more interested in her young daughter Ginny (played by Doctor Who star Mary Tamm). Why he's interested in her daughter would be to give the twist away but they sort of do that themselves anyway right at the start.

I really hated this last segment to be honest. The hokey tropical setting and themes of voodoo are very anthology film and Amicus but this is rather unpleasant to be honest. You know what Kimo and his assistant are up to very early on and nothing is done to pull the rug out from the viewer at all. Everything then follows exactly as you expect it to with no great revelatory moment or surprise. The ending is signposted early on and more than that it's an annoying ending too. I wanted the tables turned on Kimo in the EC Comics nasty people meeting a nasty end tradition but it doesn't happen. There is an explanation for the motivation of Kimo and his assistant but it still doesn't wash. Loathed this segment and I found it quite distasteful in places. Another thing about segment too is that it feels too long and is boring in the end. I feel some of these stories could have been trimmed and allowed for a fifth story to be introduced.

It's a shame really that the last segment is so dull and annoying as with with one more fun story Tales That Witness Madness would have been improved a lot and not been too far behind the Amicus films in terms of entertainment. As it stands, Tales That Witness Madness is an interesting if not entirely successful attempt to make an Amicus style compendium and suffers somewhat from the tedious fourth story and the thrown together nature of the framing device. Anthology connoisseurs and fans of eccentric British cinema will certainly want to take a look at some point though, even if it is only to see Joan Collins battle a tree trunk for her husband's affections.

TOWER OF EVIL (1972)

Tower of Evil (aka Horror on Snape Island and Beyond the Fog) was directed by Jim O'Connolly. This film was apparently rewritten a lot as it entered production and was made quite quickly. Though set on some spooky lighthouse rocks (Snape Island) out at sea it was made almost entirely on sets at Shepperton Studios and only had one day of location filming. There is some typically bad and unconvincing back projection of the era in a scene where the characters are on their way to the lighthouse in a boat. The plot begins with sailors John Gurney (George Coulouris) and his son Hamp (Jack Watson) arriving at Snape Island and finding a number of dead bodies.

A terrified young woman named Penny (Candace Glendenning) emerges and stabs Gurney. Penny is taken back to the mainland and has gone catatonic. Dr Simpson (Anthony Valentine), with the aid of some flashing disco lights, attempts to make Penny dredge up her repressed memories of the bloodbath on the island. Anyway, a team of scientists decide to visit the island because they believe it is stuffed with gold and Phoenician treasure. Oh, and a private detective named Brent (Bryant Halliday) tags along because he has been hired to prove that Penny didn't murder her friends. Gurney goes too and seems to know more about Snape Island than he is willing to divulge. Are you keeping up with this so far? It is probably fair to say that Tower of Evil's plot is a bit more convoluted than it needed to be. It's like a mixture of Scooby-Doo and Death Line - only at sea!

The opening sequence in Tower of Evil where Gurney and his father investigate Snape Island in the fog and encounter the aftermath of a brutal bloodbath is terrific. We also get little snatches of what happened to Penny and her friends in flashbacks which play a lot like a slasher film - which makes Tower of Evil somewhat ahead of its time. These flashbacks are good fun as the four young Americans (which include a dubbed Robin Askwith) smoke 'grass' and wander around naked. The problem is that this little film within a film looks more entertaining than the film we actually get - which is a group of scientists on Snape Island bickering and annoying each other as they grope towards uncovering the secrets of these cursed rocks. I actually love the framing sequence of Anthony Valentine and his crazy disco lights trying to restore Penny's memories but this is quickly forgotten and dispensed with in the film. It's sort of like Tower of Evil had enough ideas for three different films and only fragments of two of these ideas remain.

Tower of Evil has some fairly basic sets to depict Snape Island but it does have some gruesome deaths and gore which is atypical for a British horror film of this era. It also has more nudity and suggestive dialogue than one is used to from early 1970s British films. The depiction of the younger characters is amusingly dated and dubious in the way they wear clothes which seem to have been shrunk in the wash, call money 'dough' or 'bread' and are obsessed with jazz festivals. It is the scientist characters though who have the lion's share of the screen time. A problem with the male characters here is that they are too similar and so there isn't anyone to provide a contrast - save for Gary Hamilton's young Brom. Bryant Haliday (a late addition to the cast) is a decent lead and Australian actor Mark Edwards is the urbane and patronising Adam. A nuclear bomb could off at Snape Island and Adam would just shrug and dispense a dry aside. Yes Minister star Derek Fowlds, who was Mr Derek in Basil Brush around this time, is fairly dull as the irritable Dan Winthrop.

Anna Palk is part of the expedition as Nora. Nora wears an outfit that leaves nothing to the imagination and also gets high to relieve the boredom. Jill Haworth, already a horror veteran, plays Rose Mason. Jack Watson lends solid support as the mysterious but decent boat captain John Gurney. I spent much of this film trying to work out what accent Watson is trying to do. Answers on a postcard please. I was rather disappointed that Anthony Valentine and Candace Glendenning barely featured in the film after being established at the beginning and I think I would have liked more of the scenes featuring the young Americans on Snape Island. If you'd turned that film within a film into a feature length film and called it Bloodbath on Snape Island you'd have had a cheesy cult classic I think.

Tower of Evil isn't the longest film in the world but it does feel like it drags out the central mystery longer than it needs to and becomes a bit silly near the end. It feels like they throw the kitchen sink at the film in the third act with all these crazy reveals and things blowing up. I'm not sure you really needed all of this because the locale is atmospheric and a good constrictive setting for a simple horror thriller. Not to say I didn't enjoy Tower of Evil because by and large I had a good time. The premise is interesting and the blood drenched kills are excellent. The cave sets near the end are fun too because they shared some of these sets with the framing sequence for the Amicus film Tales from the Crypt.

My frustration with Tower of Evil is that it seems to lack focus and has way too many tangents and characters - some of which get discarded and forgotten. This film could have done with a tighter focus and a more streamlined story. Tower of Evil is probably less than the sum of its parts on the whole but it is an interesting film with some very effective moments of horror and practical gore effects. I gather the original cinema cut of this film was (ahem) slashed to pieces by the censors and had to remove some nudity, a gory death scene, and even the sequence near the end where someone is on fire. Happily though you can now watch Tower of Evil in all of its blood splattered and nude glory.

TROG (1970)

Did you know that Joan Crawford's real name was Lucille LeSueur? She hated the name Joan Crawford but it was imposed on her by the studio. The studio thought that LeSueur sounded too much like sewer. Bette Davis and Joan Crawford famously had a fierce rivalry and tense relationship. After the death of Crawford in 1977, Bette Davis said - "You should never say bad things about the dead, you should only say good. Joan Crawford is dead. Good." Davis once famously joked that Joan Crawford had slept with every star on the MGM lot except Lassie. I've no idea why I started this review with some trivia but you have to start somewhere and with Trog it is difficult to know exactly where to start.

This was the last film Joan Crawford ever made. Trog was directed by Freddie Francis and takes place in present day England. A cave is found to contain a troglodyte which may be the missing link between apes and humans. How the troglodyte survived in this cave is not certain. Presumably he just popped down to Asda when he was out of food. The local folks are not too happy about this discovery but an impeccably dressed anthropologist named Dr Brockton (played by Lucille LeSueur, sorry, I mean Joan Crawford) takes charge of the situation with her tranquilizer gun. Dr Brockton takes 'Trog' back to her lab and is soon teaching it how to play catch and wear neckscarves. I'd imagine they probably sneaked in a few games of Connect 4 too. Trouble is brewing though in the form of local businessman Sam Murdock (Michael Gough). Murdock thinks that a troglodyte living in the area is going to be bad for business. He is determined to get rid of 'Trog' and foil the research of Dr Brockton.

Trog is one of the daftest films turned out by the British horror film industry in the 1970s and that's really saying something because there were a lot of daft horror films in that decade. What has made this film endearing, even cultish today, is the fact that Joan Crawford seems to be taking it seriously. Though she has been reduced to appearing in this low-budget horror film her professional pride and dignity makes Joan determined to give it her all nonetheless as if this is a serious dramatic role which might somehow net her a surprise twilight Oscar. So you get this strange situation where you have Joan Crawford playing it straight while acting alongside a man in a ridiculous monkey mask wearing what look like Ugg boots. The man in the monkey suit is Joe Cornelius, who was actually a wrestler for many years. Legend has it that the monkey suit in this film was a leftover from Kubrick's 2001.

Dr Brockton teaches Trog tricks in the manner that you would a dog. They roll a ball to one another outside. Trog has the makings of a decent goalkeeper if you ask me. He's a quick learner. The suspension of disbelief required for this film is not helped by the Trog costume. It is clearly just a man in rags with a monkey head slapped on him. The monkey mask is not convincing and Joe Cornelius looks like he can barely move his head in that get-up. Trog grunts and growls a lot as Dr Brockton encourages and chides him in the same fashion that Barbara Woodhouse would a disobedient labrador. There's a bit of Frankenstein and King Kong in the story. Dr Brockton is eager to see how much of a capacity for intelligence and learning Trog has. I don't know what her ultimate goal is. Perhaps she wants him to become the world's first troglodyte airline pilot.

One of the (strange) highlights of the film is when Trog has a flashback - which is depicted by a stop-motion dinosaur sequence. This was old stock footage originally produced by Willis O'Brien and Ray Harryhausen. Trog is a baffling and terrible film but I suppose it does cross some sort of strange threshold where it becomes quite entertaining merely by dint of being so rubbish. This is one of those films where you have no idea why anyone thought it would be a good idea to make it the first place. The fact that Joan Crawford agreed to star in it merely adds to its strange charm. Oddly, the basic plot of Trog is not dissimilar to a 1984 film called Iceman - where a prehistoric Neanderthal caveman is brought back to life and studied by a scientist. Iceman is a pretty good film though - which can't be said of Trog.

There are a smattering of familiar faces in the film. Michael

Gough teams up with Joan again (after Beserk!) as Murdock and look out for David Warbeck and Chloe Franks in this film too. Chloe Franks was a child actor and appeared in a couple of Amicus films after Trog. Trog is one of those films which people only watch these days for a few laughs. This is an utterly preposterous film but if you like Joan Crawford this is a piece of history as it was her last performance in a feature film. Joan's fetching biege pantsuits alone make Trog worth a look.

UNDERWORLD (1985)

Underworld was directed by George Pavlou and written by Clive Barker and James Caplin. It was re-titled as Transmutations for the American release. This was an original script Barker wrote after agreeing to participate on a film with George Pavlou. The script got changed a lot though and Barker washed his hands of the film. His original concept was more of a noir film featuring mobsters and monsters. You get gangsters and monsters in the film but it is made in more of 80s pop video style than noir. Clive Barker thought this was an awful film and I think you'd struggle to find anyone willing to disagree with that.

Barker was still foolish enough though to let Pavlou have a crack at Rawhead Rex straight after this. As George W. Bush once wisely said, Fool me once, shame on... shame on you. Fool me, er, you can't get fooled again. Anyway, what is the plot of Underworld? Well, it has something to do with a high class hooker named Nicole (Nicola Cowper) being kidnapped by monsters. A powerful man named Hugo (Steven Berkoff) wants Nicole back and hires Roy (Larry Lamb) to find her. Roy is an old flame of Nicole or something. To cut to the chase, this all revolves around a powerful drug which turns people into mutants. The key figure when it comes to this drug is Dr Savary (Denholm Elliott)...

You stumble into Underworld in the hope that it might be a cheesily enjoyable 80s horror film with some scares and fun but sadly none of that transpires in the end. This is an incredibly boring film where nothing seems to happen for long stretches of the running time. The music in the film is by Freur - who later named themselves after this film and became Underworld. That's a nice piece of trivia. Sadly though, the music by 'Freur' in this film will have you stuffing bog roll in your ears. One thing that is interesting about Underground (the film that is, not the band, this is getting confusing) is that Barker's fondness for sympathetic monsters, displayed in his 1990 film Nightbreed, is very apparent here despite all the changes to the script.

Nightbreed is more like the film that Barker probably wanted Underground to be - which is unsurprising given that he directed Nightbreed. Barker actually turned down an offer to write and direct Alien 3 in the early 1990s because he wasn't interested in the xenomorphs. He likes his monsters to be a bit more complex. Miranda Richardson was somehow roped into appearing in Underworld, as too was Phil Davis but he isn't in it for very long. Denholm Elliott is definitely slumming it somewhat appearing in this film. The same year (1985) he got an Oscar nomination for A Room with a View. Steven Berkoff does his usual thing and you get Art Malik, Ingrid Pitt, and Brian Croucher. Look out too for Hellraiser star Sean Chapman.

It would be fibbing though to say that George Pavlou had drawn memorable performances from these familiar names. Most of them don't seem to have the faintest idea what they are even doing here in the first place. Nicola Cowper is at least decent though as Nicole. This film bombed heavily when it came out and quickly scurried away into complete obscurity. The only reason people watch it today is because they become curious due to the Clive Barker link. You'll notice though that, unlike other horror films which did poorly on release but built a cult following years later, there is still literally no one demanding for Underworld be rediscovered and given some overdue love.

The version of Underworld titled Transmutations for the American market has fifteen extra minutes of material so you should perhaps watch that version - although an extra fifteen minutes of this film doesn't sound especially attractive to me. The original version feels long enough as it is. The weird thing about Underworld is that you'd think the passage of time would have lent it some retro charm or a novelty factor but it really hasn't. This is just a very dull and badly made film. Underworld seems to ration a lot of its budget for the big action showdown at the end but by that stage you'll probably be fast asleep anyway. I'm definitely not a fan of this film and I didn't like Rawhead Rex either. The only good thing about these two films is that it motivated Clive Barker to take full creative control on Hellraiser.

UNMAN, WITTERING AND ZIGO (1971)

Unman, Wittering and Zigo was directed by John Mackenzie. It was adapted by Simon Raven from Giles Cooper's 1958 BBC Radio 3 radio drama of the same name. You'd probably describe this as more of a thriller than a horror film but it does have a horror sort of feel and atmosphere at times. In the film, a young teacher named John Ebony (David Hemmings) arrives at Chantry School to take up a new teaching position in the middle of term. Chantry School is an austere posh old-fashioned sort of place where they have Latin lessons rather than woodwork. Ebony moves into a cottage at the school with his wife Silvia (Carolyn Seymour). He is replacing Mr Pelham - a teacher who died in mysterious circumstances after falling off a cliff (this film is supposed to be set in Cornwall I believe and the school is near the sea). Mr Ebony is full of idealism and enthusiasm for his new post. He probably thinks he's going to be like Robin Williams in Dead Poet's Society. It doesn't quite turn out that way though.

Mr Ebony soon learns that his class of pupils are rebellious to say the least. They treat Ebony with polite disdain and even patronise him. The pupils suggest to Ebony that Mr Pelham's death was not an accident and that they murdered him. They tell Mr Ebony that he will end up meeting the same fate if he doesn't comply with their instructions. They order Mr Ebony to give them good grades and also force him to place bets at the bookies for them. No one in the school seems to believe Ebony when he mentions the pupils claiming they murdered Pelham. Not even Ebony's wife believes him. She just laughs. Ebony decides he will solve the mystery of Mr Pelham's death and refuses to buckle to these young bullies...

Unman, Wittering and Zigo (a reference to the last names on the class register) is a very gripping film although the ending is slightly disappointing. I don't really know why this film isn't better known. The title definitely doesn't help though. The school in the film is one of daily prayers, old duffer teachers, soldier cadet training and war games, and homoeroticism. The school is an obvious metaphor for Britain in that decade and how it needs to be thoroughly shaken up and altered to drag it into changing times,

The film highlights the anachronistic nature of these public school institutions with their centuries old customs, still attempting to instill the fear of God, snobbishness and strict Victorian military bearing into schoolboys when Britain and the world has changed - and still is changing - far more than the stuffy, claustrophobic confines of the school will apparently ever seem willing to acknowledge. This film is not a fan of posh boarding schools and seems to suggest they breed sociopaths. I've never been inside a posh boarding school in my life so I couldn't really tell you how accurate the film is in depicting one.

David Hemmings, in the days before his eyebrows took over like that green fungus on Stephen King in Creepshow, is very good in the film. Mr Ebony is in a difficult position because if he simply beats the crap out of these blackmailing kids it will be him that gets into trouble. So he has to find a way to outwit them. I must say I did enjoy the scene where Mr Ebony has some beans on toast and Hemmings simply pushes the beans around his plate with a fork for about five minutes. He definitely didn't want to eat those beans. I can't act AND eat beans at the same time! Carolyn Seymour, who has been in many things (Star Trek, Babylon 5, Quantum Leap etc) but for me will always be Zita the stripper in the first Steptoe & Son film, is really good too as Ebony's wife. The darkest scene in the film comes when the boys, in order to keep Mr Ebony in line, lure his wife to the gym at night and basically threaten to rape her. This is a tense and well shot sequence.

I really like Tony Haygarth in this film too as an easygoing teacher who Mr Ebony comes to confide in. Douglas Wilmer also hits the right notes as the snooty and remote headmaster. One problem with this film, and it is not an uncommon one as far as old films set in schools go, is that some of the pupils in Ebony's class look more like middle-aged men than schoolboys. They were definitely pushing it casting some of these actors as schoolboys. There are some familiar faces playing the boys. Michael Kitchen, with a big mop of hair, is one of them and also Tom Owen. Tom Owen, many years later, became best known for his role as Compo's long lost son in Last of the Summer Wine. I also recognised

David Jackson in this film. Jackson was one of the escaped lunatics in Killer's Moon. By the way, look out for Barbara Lott in this film too. She was later in the sitcom Sorry! as Ronnie Corbett's overbearing and barking mad mother. Language,

Timothy! Unman, Wittering and Zigo is a surprisingly gripping thriller on the whole and, despite being a long film, kept me engaged right to the end. This is certainly a film that deserves more recognition than it ever attained.

UNMASKED PART 25 (1988)

Unmasked Part 25 (aka The Hand of Death) was directed by Anders Palm and written by Mark Cutforth. This is a very obscure film and went straight to video in 1988. Unmasked Part 25 is a meta horror film that blends horror, drama, melodrama, and comedy. It actually reminded me somewhat of the 2006 film Behind the Mask: The Rise of Leslie Vernon. Both of these films have a similar sort of premise. The premise is basically something like this - what does Jason Vorhees do in his spare time when he isn't killing people and what is he like in private? Unmasked Part 25 revolves around Jackson (Gregory Cox). Jackson is a serial killer in London who wears a hockey mask. We learn that he grew up in the United States but left after an incident at a summer camp. He's basically supposed to be Jason Vorhees but they obviously can't use that name so he's Jackson instead.

After murdering a bunch of people at some swanky party, Jackson meets a blind woman named Shelly (Fiona Evans). Fiona is kind and understanding to Jackson and they begin a romance. We learn that Jackson is tired of being a serial killer and going through something akin to a midlife crisis. Jackson is especially dismayed by the endless sequels in a horror franchise named Hand of Death - which were clearly based on him...

Unmasked Part 25 begins with some brutal kills (one chap has his face ripped off) by Jackson which feature some excellent gore effects. You can see the people who made this film were big fans of the slasher genre and the legendary practical effects work done by the likes of Tom Savini. The film then spins on its axis and becomes a melodrama with Jackson bemoaning his destiny in life to be a killer who everyone regards to be a monster. There is also comedy in the film too and therein lies the main problem with this film. It never quite seems to work out what it wants to be and tonally is all over the place. This does make it a unique sort of experience but some stretches of the film are a bit boring and frustrating while other parts are really good. This film is what you could describe then as a mixed bag.

The plot arc where Shelly and Jackson have a romance feels very inspired by The Toxic Avenger. Six Characters in Search of an Author by Luigi Pirandello is is often cited as an influence on this film too. Gregory Cox is good as the Vorhees type character. When he takes his mask off he has a mangled monstrous face in the tradition of Friday the 13th. Fiona Evans (who doesn't seem to have done much acting outside of this film) is also decent as Shelly. There aren't really any familiar faces in the film although Edward Brayshaw, who pops up here, was an Australian actor who did loads of stuff. He was Harold Meaker in Rentaghost. The victim named Barry in the film was played by the late Christian Brando - who was the son of Marlon Brando.

Unmasked Part 25 is generally a likeable and interesting effort. It is something a bit different and offers an effective postmodern twist on the slasher genre. Doing a genuine horror comedy is not easy (I would say things like Return of the Living Dead and Evil Dead II are the best examples of getting this tricky blend of horror and comedy right) and Unmasked Part 25 is not entirely successful but it's a decent effort all the same. I did find my interest starting to flag when the romance plot kicks in and you may find the scenes where Jackson visits his dad a bit boring. The general idea here is to get some backstory on Jackson and find out where a Jason Vorhees style maniac comes from and what makes them tick. Do they enjoy their grisly work? Unmasked Part 25 is uneven but worth a look purely for the undiluted slasher homages alone. This film would probably make a good double bill with Behind the Mask: The Rise of Leslie Vernon.

WHAT WAITS BELOW (1984)

What Waits Below (aka Secrets of the Phantom Caverns) was directed by Don Sharp. It might be pushing things to call this a horror film but you do get snake monsters and some gore here and there. The middle half of the film is a lot like a horror film but then it veers off more into sci-fi with some Mole Men and Time Machine (and maybe even Beneath the Planet of the Apes) style influences. It ends up a bit like one of those Doug McClure Amicus films or an especially daft episode of Doctor Who and yet everything is played straight and taken seriously so you don't get any campiness to mitigate the film's flaws. The director Don Sharp wasn't a fan of this film and, realising he had a stinker on his hands, left the project before it was edited. You can picture him sneaking out of the studio with a giant fake beard after viewing a rough cut.

The story takes place in Central America and revolves around the American military testing a new type of super powerful transmitter in a large cave system. When they lose contact with the transmitter a team has to be sent in to investigate what happened. Caving expert Rupert 'Wolf' Wolfsen (Robert Powell), scientists Leslie Peterson (Lisa Blount) and Ben Gannon (Richard Johnson) are part of the team but their patience is tested by the bad tempered and annoying expedition leader Major Elbert Stevens (Timothy Bottoms). They soon have other concerns too when it becomes increasingly apparent that they aren't alone in these caves.

What Waits Below is sometimes compared to Neil Marshall's The Descent but I'd lower those expectations if you decide to watch this film. What Waits Below is a fairly lifeless and cheap film that does become something of a slog at times. They shot a lot of the film in real caves in the United States - which was apparently something they soon regretted due to the logistical problems. Though the bulk of the film takes place in caves the characters in What Waits Below are nearly always in wide open spaces when underground. This surely defeats the object of making a thriller set in some caves. There is no tension or sense of claustrophobia. Some of the cave backdrops are interesting but there is no sense of wonder because everything is shot like a drab television film.

The start of the film is quite good fun because there is a jungle action chase like something out of The A-Team and the early sections in the caves are not bad either because there are fleeting glimpses of things lurking in the shadows. This builds up some intrigue which is gradually dissipated by the sedate and samey quality of the film and then the big reveal of the risible albino underground dwellers. There is actually a decent cast in What Waits Below but sadly they all seem like they'd rather be doing something else. Robert Powell is not very convincing as the Milk Tray Man style cave expert and adventurer 'Wolf' Wolfsen and sensibly decides to underplay his part and just get through this experience with his dignity intact. Wolf wears jeans and a leather jacket on the expedition and is improbably depicted as being sexually irresistible to Lisa Blount's scientist Leslie.

Richard Johnson, with that rich thespy mature voice which makes him sound like he's doing a commercial for Werther's Originals, seems a bit bored in What Waits Below but he's a professional and does what is required of him. Timothy Bottoms has the most thankless task in the film as the no nonsense military villain Major Stevens. Bottoms never goes as bonkers as you want him to. What this film really needed to liven it up was a bit more scenery chewing from someone. Timothy Bottoms was in films like The Last Picture Show and The Paper Chase in the 1970s but by 1984 his career was clearly on the skids. The venerable Anne Heywood is also part of the expedition as Frieda and genuinely seems to have no idea what this film is about or why her agent has booked her in it. This was the last film she ever made although she did do some television afterwards. The last ever credit of Anne Heywood was The Equalizer: The Mystery of Manon. There's some trivia that will be of no use to you whatsoever.

What Waits Below is definitely an odd film which never quite seems to work out what it wants to be. It starts as an action caper, flirts with being a horror film, and then becomes a daft sci-fi B picture. I'm always happy to give a cave themed horror film a go so I was disappointed that What Waits Below didn't lean in on this angle a lot more. A character is attacked by fanged puppet snake rock monsters at one point and the film suddenly becomes fun. Sadly though it soon departs from this sort of stuff. The chap attacked by snake monsters doesn't even get eaten. They just bandage his arm up! There are a few grisly moments here and there but on the whole What Waits Below is a fairly dull film with a silly (and not in a good way) third act. What Waits Below doesn't really offer anything new or novel to the cave fantasy/horror genre - aside perhaps from the lead hero having the name Rupert.

THE WICKER TREE (2011)

The Wicker Tree was directed by Robin Hardy and was based on his novel Cowboys For Christ. This is basically a sequel to Robin Hardy's 1973 classic The Wicker Man although it was described by Hardy as more of a companion piece. The Wicker Man is one of the greatest horror films ever made while The Wicker Tree is one of the worst horror films ever made. It's true what they say. You can never go home again and Robin Hardy should have deduced that for himself before embarking on this fiasco. This wretched sequel is an amateurish waste of everyone's time. The ludicrous story has two young American

Christians named Steve (Henry Garrett) and Beth Boothby (Britannia Nicol) sent to 'heathen' Scotland to teach them about God. They end up being invited to a village by Sir Lachlan Morrison (Graham McTavish) and, well, if you've seen the original film, you'll have a good idea of what eventually happens.

The two leads in The Wicker Tree can't act to save their lives and the film plays like cheap student film shot with a camcorder. Henry Garrett, who plays Steve, is actually English in real life. I have no idea who Britannia Nicol is when she's at home. The Wicker Tree is her only acting credit. It is certainly a bit of a drop in quality (to say the least) to go from Edward Woodward to Britannia Nicol as your lead actor. Most of the actors here seem embarrassed and aware that they've ended up in a real stinker. Christopher Lee was going to be the lead of the film but had to pull out because of illness. Lucky for him really. He has a cameo instead with the lead villain role going to Graham McTavish. McTavish is always reliable but he isn't in the film enough. I gather that Joan Collins was going to be in the film alongside Christopher Lee but when he pulled out they replaced Joan with the younger Jacqueline Leonard (as Delia Morrison).

Nothing in this terrible film makes much sense and it's little wonder that it didn't find a theatrical release. The notion that Scotland is some primitive backwater is preposterous for a film made in 2011. The pagan cult mumbo jumbo just seems tiresome and silly here. In the original film it was fascinating, mysterious, entrancing, and scary. Former child actor and Foyle's War star Honeysuckle Weeks is cast in the film as Lolly - a villager who is irresistible to men apparently. I suppose you could say she's sort of pitched loosely as the Britt Ekland of this film. The Wicker Tree's determination to have Honeysuckle Weeks nude as often as possible becomes downright weird in the end. Lolly goes skinny dipping in a river at one point despite the fact it looks flaming freezing.

That poor girl is going to end up with hypothermia.

There are a smattering of familiar faces in the film. Clive Russell (who was, among other things, Brynden 'Blackfish' Tully in Game of Thrones) pops up in a comic role as the butler. It feels like the actors here liked the idea of being in a new Wicker Man film with Christopher Lee but then ended up in something which they probably would have avoided had they known how bad it was going to be. There is a bit of gore in The Wicker Man but it isn't ever scary or unsettling like the first film. The last act tries to subvert some of the expectations you might have from your knowledge of The Wicker Man but you'll probably be past caring by then. The cult group in this film worship the deity Sulis but you'll be so bored they might as well be worshiping Basil Brush. In fact, that probably would have been more entertaining.

What this film illustrates perfectly is how the original Wicker Man was lightning in a bottle. You just can't replicate the wonderfully strange and chilling nature of that brilliant 'folk horror' film. Robin Hardy (who hardly made any films in between these two Wicker Man pictures) should really have left The Wicker Man to stand alone as an undoubted classic of British cinema. If you do love the original it is best to pretend that The Wicker Tree doesn't exist.

XTRO TRILOGY (1922-1995)

Xtro is a cultishly bizarre 1982 sci-fi horror film directed by Harry Bromley Davenport. It isn't really a forgotten horror film because it is quite famous in cult circles and pops up on telly quite a bit (or at least it used to). The rarely seen second and third Xtro films though are definitely perfect fodder for this book. Anyway, in the first Xtro a man is kidnapped by a UFO and three years later returns (a woman gives birth to him fully grown in a famously disgusting scene) to be with his son and estranged wife but - naturally - he isn't quite the man that he used to be. Xtro is often jumbled in with Alien clones thanks to the birth scene and a few moments of extraterrestrial horror (the alien creature seen in the road by the woods at night is rather creepy) but, generally, there aren't a huge amount of similarities despite this often appearing on lists of films that were inspired by Alien. The most obvious Alien homages are a facehugger (of sorts) in one of the endings and alien eggs.

Xtro is really only for those who enjoy surreal and strange low-budget horror films. Not an awful lot makes any sense here and the director Harry Bromley Davenport has candidly admitted in interviews that Xtro was never meant to have narrative logic or any coherence. They were more or less making it up as they went along. It was merely meant to be disgusting and make some money (and succeeded on both of those counts). Some of the more nonsensical and bizarre flourishes in the film were apparently included at the behest of the producer. This jumble of scenes and images is jarring and confusing but might account for its mild cult status. Where else are you going to see a film where a life size Action Man toy bayonets an old lady to death? Xtro is probably best summed up by the fact that three different endings were shot and none of them make any sense whatsoever. If you do watch Xtro look out for future Bond girl Maryam d'Abo and Lou Beale from EastEnders. I can't say I've ever been the biggest fan of Xtro but it is probably something that every British horror fan should at least take a gander at.

Xtro II: The Second Encounter is 1990 sequel to Xtro and had Harry Bromley Davenport back in the director's chair. Davenport only made the film though because he needed the money. This one has no connection to the original Xtro (Bromley Davenport did not have the rights to the Xtro story but he had the legal rights to the Xtro name) and was made in Canada (though still a British co-production). They look as if they spent even less money on this one than Xtro. At least in the original they had some outdoor location work. Xtro II is a rip-off of both Alien and James Cameron's Aliens. The film is set in an underground government research base where experiments into other dimensions take place. When a creature from another dimension becomes at large in the base a group of soldiers and scientists must fight for survival. Xtro II is a very bargain basement Aliens but also references Alien. Yet again in one of these Alien franchise clones we get creature bursting from someone's chest at the start.

Xtro II is one of those cheap science fiction horror films that sounds a lot more entertaining on paper than it actually is to watch. The entire film takes place in what looks like a warehouse and you only see the alien creature a few times (it is slimy and vaguely Gigeresque). Xtro II is always battling its non existent budget and the lack of money ultimately sinks the film. Well, that and some truly atrocious acting from the cast. The only famous name on offer is Airwolf star Jan Michael Vincent. Vincent genuinely looks as if he has no idea what he's doing in this film. He barely looks as if he's awake and his disinterest is all too apparent. Harry Bromley Davenport later said that he had to read out the lines to Vincent before each scene because the actor never bothered to read the script. Watching the film and Jan Michael Vincent's performance, that news doesn't come as a huge surprise. Xtro II is a scraping from the bottom of the barrel as far as Alien franchise rip-off films go and never offers sufficient horror or action to keep the viewer interested. Ultimately, the clear absence of any budget completely torpedoes the film.

In 1995, Harry Bromley Davenport optimistically decided the world was ready for yet more Xtro capers and released Xtro 3: Watch the Skies - which wasn't a British production unlike the first two. This is slightly more watchable than Xtro II but that's not exactly a big achievement. The story in this one has a squad of marines trapped on an island with a vengeful alien who was captured and experimented on at a secret facility. There are riffs on Alien and Aliens but the film that Xtro 3 rips off the most is Predator. As with the first Xtro sequel, Harry Bromley Davenport is hamstrung by a minuscule budget (you have to wait forever for any action in this film and even when it does arrive it seems small scale and inept) and an amatuerish cast who bark at each other and give embarrassing performances. There is though a cameo by Robert Culp as an army general. How on earth did they persuade Robert Culp to appear in this? They must have blown half the budget on his fee. Xtro 3 is largely a waste of time (save perhaps for a slightly surreal sequence when they stumble across some alien technology conveyed by lights and laser beams) and only for curious Xtro completists (if there even is such a thing).

THE YOUNG POISONER'S HANDBOOK (1995)

The Young Poisoner's Handbook is a great little film from 1995 directed by Benjamin Ross. The film revolves around Graham Young (Hugh O'Conor), a high IQ misfit and introverted outsider who develops a remarkable scientific ability and fascination from a very young age. The story begins in 1961 with Graham fourteen years-old and living a fairly dull life in the working class suburbia of Neasden with his dysfunctional television obsessed parents (played Ruth Sheen and Roger Lloyd Pack) and very annoying older sister Winnie (the late Charlotte Coleman). Graham, who has a very strange sense of himself and the world, is vaguely repulsed by his family and spends most of his time in his bedroom conducting elaborate chemistry experiments in the hope of somehow creating a diamond. After putting antimony sulphide in his vials he inadvertently produces a lethal toxin which he soon becomes obsessed by. Rapidly discovering new things about the world of toxins all the time, Graham dreams about becoming the most brilliant poisoner of all time and decides the first test case will be his awful stepmother...

The Young Poisoner's Handbook is loosely based on the story of the real life Graham Young * who became known as the 'Teacup Poisoner' for his somewhat anti-social activities in the sixties and early seventies. The real Young though was a more prosaic character, just a plain nutcase and obsessed with Nazis. The Graham Young in this film is, understandably for cinematic purposes, very different and brilliantly played by Hugh O'Conor. O'Conor's Graham Young is a genius, outwardly courteous, gentle and well spoken (with a very dry sense of humour) and strangely rather likeable. The only problem is that the coldly calculating Graham, with his wide-eyed scientific curiosity, has no heart or emotions whatsoever and is far more concerned with his ongoing chemical experiments than the welfare of individual human beings. "Life is a series of illusions that only a scientist could strip away," reflects Graham with his clinical view of everything.

It is only when Graham tries to poison his father that he is caught and sent to Harshhurst Hospital, an institution for the criminally insane. Oddly, Graham wants to be caught for the notoriety and fame, a crucial thing for the curriculum vitae of any great poisoner in his own estimation. Deemed fit to re-enter society several years later by the liberal and trendy dream analysing prison psychiatrist Dr Zeigler (Anthony Sher), Graham is fixed up with a menial job as a storekeeper at a small, cheerful, photographic laboratory. The question of how long will he be able to resist his scientific fascination with poisoning people makes for a compelling final arc to the film, especially as Graham is now placed in an environment full of opportunity and temptation with an abundance of both chemicals and people.

The Young Poisoner's Handbook is an offbeat black comedy and social satire with a sneakily malevolent wit, sort of like a cross between A Clockwork Orange and a vintage Ealing comedy. The story is certainly morbidly compelling and macabre though from very early on when Graham poisons his stepmother and keeps a meticulous scientific diary charting her progress as he experiments and tinkers with the dosage. This is probably the darkest portion of the film but The Young Poisoner's Handbook always offsets its subject matter with a very genteel British atmosphere and a sly sense of humour. Plus, his stepmother is so unpleasant your sympathy leans towards Graham here - "You contaminate everything you touch. I'm going to scrub you till you are raw!" Although The Young Poisoner's Handbook is set in a very down to earth English suburbia, it maintains a slightly heightened reality and an offbeat quality that lifts it well above the numerous abysmal British films made on the back on Lottery money from the nineties onwards. This is a film that deserved a much wider audience and following.

The Young Poisoner's Handbook also paints an effectively dull portrait of ordinary sixties working class life and interestingly conveys the gradual social shifts of the time as it moves into the somewhat more kitsch seventies. The film is essentially three acts, consisting of Graham's early experiments with his family, his time in prison and then his release. The prison section is possibly the only part of the film that might slightly sag or seem a trifle familiar to some viewers although it's always absorbing as Graham befriends the pioneering psychiatrist Zeigler and persuades the authorities that he is now completely sane and cured. The Young Poisoner's Handbook seems to be critical in particular of trendy psychiatrists playing God and deciding when some sociopath or murderer is suitable to be released back into society.

Having Graham lumbered with a job in brown overalls for which he is, of course, ridiculously too intelligent, provides some funny little moments and The Young Poisoner's Handbook does a great job in capturing the sometimes lairy and often tedious banter of a small factory type environment where everybody thinks they are a comedian. The misanthropic Graham's attempts to fit into his new job without standing out too much make for compelling viewing and the third act really amps up the tension as Graham goes about his dull job, which includes serving everybody a mug of tea!

There is a great little moment where Graham is waiting to be interviewed for the job and sighs heavily when a youngster next to him complains that the job will be impossible to get because the employer wants O'Levels - as if that was some preposterously out of reach qualification that no mere mortal could ever aspire to. There is also another amusing moment when Graham starts questioning a police scientific expert and proves considerably more knowledgeable, much to the bewilderment of the older man. O'Conor gives a very compelling and impressive performance as Graham and his emotionless and analytical narration throughout the film is spot-on. The Young Poisoner's Handbook will probably not appeal to everyone, but this is a dark, amusing and very entertaining film that deserves more of a cult following.

* The real Graham Young was born in Neasden in Middlesex on the 7th of September 1947. As a youth he became obsessed with poisons and chemicals and decided to conduct some experiments of his own. The unwitting guinea pigs in these experiments were his own family. Young's usual method was to lace drinks like tea with thallium and antimony. Thallium can affect your nervous system, lung, heart, liver, and kidney if large amounts are eaten or drunk for short periods of time. Temporary hair loss, vomiting, and diarrhea can also occur and death may result after exposure to large amounts of thallium for short periods. Young began poisoning his stepmother, father, and sister in 1961. He managed to obtain potentially dangerous chemicals from a chemist by pretending to be older than he actually was. Soon, everyone around Graham Young seemed to be suffering from dreadful stomach pains - even including some pupils at his school.

The family began to have suspicions about Graham Young but

they couldn't find any firm evidence and he naturally denied everything (Young actually blamed his sister). When his mother died it was put down to a medical complaint. Graham (of course) took the chance to slip some poison into food at his mother's funeral. By now, suspicions about Graham Young and his activities were spreading beyond the family. One of his teachers (who found poisonous chemicals in Young's desk) suspected he was up to something dangerous. The police became involved and Young was found to have thallium and antimony in his possession. He confessed to secretly administering poison to his family and a school friend. Young was sent to Broadmoor - where he was the youngest inmate for many years. He was charged with killing his stepmother.

Graham Young spent nine years at Broadmoor. It is alleged that he may even have killed someone at Broadmoor by extracting poison from laurel bush leaves in the gardens. When he was released from Broadmoor in 1971, Young soon went back to his old ways. He somehow managed to purchase antimony potassium tartrate and thallium from a chemist. While attending a storekeeping course in Slough, Young poisoned a man named Trevor Sparkes more than once. Sparkes did not die but he was violently ill from his ordeal. Graham Young then secured a job at John Hadland Laboratories in Bovingdon, Hertfordshire. Broadmoor provided him with a reference but - amazingly - did not inform John Hadland Laboratories that Young was a convicted poisoner! One of Young's duties at the lab was to push the tea trolley around. Talk about a recipe for disaster! You can probably guess what happened next.

Very soon a mysterious 'bug' at the lab had everyone coming down with dreadful stomach pains. It was later established that Young would actually poison people as a way of gaining promotion. Bob Egle died as a result of poisoning and Ron Hewitt left the firm after falling ill. As a consequence of this respective death and departure, Graham Young was promoted to head storeroom clerk. Young would keep diaries of his activities and keep abreast of how his various poisonings were affecting the victims. If anyone was rude to him he would give them a dose of poison and then note how much he was enjoying their discomfort. Young next poisoned two men named David Tilson and Jethro Batt with thalium. They both survived but suffered dreadfully. Their hair fell out and they were bedridden and deeply ill.

Fred Biggs, a 56-year-old local councillor, was the next victim. Biggs worked part time at the lab and had his tea poisoned by Young. He died as a result of the poisoning. Biggs was poisoned so badly that his skin started to peel away. By now the staff at John Hadland Laboratories had become very suspicious of Graham Young. They had deduced two very salient things. The first was that this violent and mysterious stomach bug had only began swirling around when Graham Young joined the firm. The second thing they deduced was that Graham Young never seemed to be affected! That was more than a little suspicious.

The police did a (long overdue) check on Graham Young and found out about his storied history as a prolific poisoner. They searched his home and found that he had a very large stash of poisons. They also found his diaries in which he'd written copious notes about who he had poisoned and what effects the chemicals had on them. Graham Young knew the game was up now and confessed. He even confessed to murdering his late stepmother. Graham Young was highly intelligent but deeply disturbed. The police found that his room was full of swastikas and pictures of Adolf Hitler.

Young was charged with two counts of murder, two counts of attempted murder, four counts of administering poison with intent to injure and four counts of administering poison with intent to cause grievous bodily harm. He (rather preposterously) pled not guilty and tried to claim that his diary was not real but simply a fantasy novel he was writing. This defence was predictably hopeless and he was sentenced to life in prison. Young is generally credited with at least three murders but poisoned about 80+ people. Who knows how many people he might have killed if he'd stayed in society for a few years longer. It is said that in prison Young became a friend of Ian Brady. Graham Young died in prison in 1990 at the age of 42. The cause of death was a heart attack. In 2005, a Japanese schoolgirl was arrested for poisoning her mother with thallium. She had become obsessed with the story of Graham Young after watching The Young Poisoner's Handbook.

Photo Credit

Mathew MacQuarrie

https://unsplash.com/photos/white-and-black-skull-figurine-on-black-surface-u6OnpbMuZAs

Published on October 13, 2016

Milton Keynes UK
Ingram Content Group UK Ltd.
UKHW041040121124
451094UK00002B/223